Designed Living

**What happens when
the real you meets the
real God**

To Renee,
May you know the
great joy of life
in Christ —
For His glory,
Susan Sutton
Gal. 2:20

Designer Living

What happens when the real you meets the real God

Susan Sutton
author of *A Sure Path*

CLC
PUBLICATIONS
Fort Washington, PA 19034

Designer Living

Published by CLC Publications

U.S.A.
P.O. Box 1449, Fort Washington, PA 19034

UNITED KINGDOM
CLC International (UK)
51 The Dean, Alresford, Hampshire, SO24 9BJ

© 2014 by Susan Sutton
All rights reserved. Published 2014

Printed in the United States of America

ISBN (paperback): 978-1-61958-158-6
ISBN (e-book): 978-1-61958-159-3

For Sheila, Miriam and Leslie
Thank you for praying this one through

Acknowledgements

In *The Promise* by Chaim Potok, a father of one of the main characters receives a copy of his newly published book. As father and son look at the box containing the freshly printed book, the father remarks "it is only a book. But what it means to write a book."[1]

Indeed, it means many things to write a book: vision, passion, an inspired beginning followed by months of perseverance, solitude and just plain hard work. To write a book containing spiritual truth, one adds that it means much needed prayer.

For the solitude, time and prayer required to write this book, I am deeply grateful to my husband, Louis. Thank you for once again believing in my vision for a book and for understanding the physical and emotional space that I need to write. Thank you for taking time to read the chapters. Your comments and prayers encouraged me and made this book much better.

I am also thankful for the three women who agreed to pray regularly for this book. Sheila, Miriam and Leslie, you see that I have dedicated it to you. Your prayers before the throne of grace and truth have been a necessary part of keeping this book, I trust and hope, both truthful and gracious. Sheila, thank you for giving extra time to read chapters. Your eye for detail and clarity were very helpful. I want to add a special thank you to another friend, Becky Bee. Becky, you encouraged me in the process with notes, verses, gifts of hazelnut creamer for my coffee to keep me going. You are such a joy to know!

Dave Fessenden also put his skillful eye to the manuscript and added much that was needed. Thank you, Dave. Everything you suggested was not only helpful but read with a "Yes! Of course!" Thank you for not only your good editing but your friendship.

Finally, I am very grateful to CLC for believing enough in my writing to publish another of my books. You are not only a publishing company but a mission committed to God's heart for the nations. May He continually use you for His glory in the world.

Table of Contents

Introduction

Referring to the Bible as the instruction manual of the world is something of a cliché, but the metaphor fits. Scripture is where we discover how the world is meant to work and how we are meant to live. When we begin at paragraph one, page one of the Bible, we read the phrase "In the beginning God. . . ." These are significant words for the beginning of life as we know it. You and I are not even mentioned. Only God is in the picture at this point, and He is present as the visionary designer for the world. He created the physical space we occupy and filled it with all manner of life; you and I come into the picture as the last part of His creative vision. This is a significant point as we consider how we are meant to live.

A designer takes his or her creations seriously, whether the creation is a watch, a computer or a can opener. The designer's vision includes how the creation looks, its style, color and presentation, but what matters most is how it functions. I imagine that we have all bought products which look attractive but function poorly. These products often end up in a back corner of a closet or kitchen drawer, forgotten and unused. At least they do in my house. No matter how attractive a can opener may look, with the latest designer colors on its handle, if it does not open cans with ease, it is not doing what it is meant to do.

A product is at its best when it does what it is meant to do. In the same way, we are at our best when we live as we are meant to live. The best person to tell us who we are and how we are to live is the One who both envisioned and created us. The best place to learn how we "work" is the Bible. No one has more vision and passion for us than God. We cannot read the Bible without seeing His passion and purpose in every interaction with His people. We look to the One who made us to find answers for our identity and purpose.

F. B. Meyer once wrote, "Do not look from earth towards heaven but from heaven towards earth. Let God, not man, be the standpoint of vision."[1] For this reason, we begin from the standpoint of God's vision for the newly created soul. Here is the vision: We are made to belong to the One who created us, to believe His Word and to bear His image—for now and for eternity. This is who we are. This is how we are meant to live. We know it is true, because the One who created us has said so. There is a way we are designed to live, and we are at our best when we live by this design.

Something happened, however, which made our God-designed life impossible—to live as we were originally intended. We will examine why we are unable to be who we are meant to be and live as we are meant to live, then see what our visionary and passionate Designer God has done to restore us to belonging, believing and image-bearing. In light of this, the Bible is as much a *repair* manual as it is an instruction manual.

Ultimately, this book asks a question: What happens when the real you meets the real God? The answer is real change. Although there are not section titles for the book, you will see that it flows along the elements of the question. The first chapters are concerned with the real you. They focus on discovering who we are meant to be. In the next chapters, we discover the God who pursues us and makes it possible for us to be our true selves. The final chapters focus on the real change which happens when we bring ourselves to the real God for transformation.

At the end of each chapter is an opportunity for you to go beyond my words to what God says in His Word. There are questions designed to help you reflect on the truths in each chapter and to lead you into a conversation with God about what you have read. François Fénelon writes that "God will teach you more than the most experienced Christians, and better than all the books that the world has ever seen."[2] When we come to God with an open heart and a listening ear, we discover how true these words are.

Finally, if you have read any of my other books, you know that I am a lover of quotes. I read prolifically and continue to fill journals with words from writers who are much more wise and witty than I am. This book is filled with quotes. I have learned much from spiritual mentors from the past and present.

One of my favorite quotes is attributed to a seventeenth-century nun: "Lord, you know that I know myself that I am growing older and one day will be old. Keep me from the fatal habit of thinking I must say something on every subject and on everybody's affairs. . . . With my vast store of wisdom it seems a pity not to use it all, but You know, Lord, I want a few friends at the end."[3] Isn't this great? Unlike this wise and witty nun, however, I do not even suggest a vast store of wisdom, nor do I presume to have something to say on every subject (although my friends might sometimes beg to differ on that point!). I can, in all honesty, say that I know something of life with Christ in challenging places—by this I mean physically, emotionally and spiritually challenging. I know something of digging deeply into a source of strength beyond my own. I know that self-love is still very much in the well of my soul and that I long for Christlikeness to take its place.

I can only share what God has given me, which is little compared to the wisdom and experience that He has given others. I often ask when speaking before a group that God will take the crumbs of what I share and make them bread to satisfy. He can do this, and I pray that He will do so for you in this book. My prayers echo a poem by Amy Carmichael, a wise and honest missionary from the last century:

> Take this book in Thy wounded hand,
> Jesus, Lord of Calvary;
> Let it go forth at Thy command;
> Use it as it pleaseth Thee.
>
> Dust of earth, but Thy dust, Lord,
> Blade of grass, in Thy hand a sword.
> Nothing, nothing, unless it be
> Purged and quickened, O Lord, by Thee.
>
> –Amy Carmichael[4]

1

Designed to Belong

No human being knows human beings as God does.
—Oswald Chambers[1]

So God created man in his own image. (Gen. 1:27)

My friend Leslie is a creator of beautiful things. She goes to a pottery studio once a week and comes home with new creations. I love talking with Leslie about her pottery. She has such obvious joy and interest in what she creates. Every piece begins with an image in her mind which she shapes into something tangible with her hands. When she has finished, the new creation bears not only her unique style but also her unique signature. Even without the special design of her name etched onto each piece, no one would challenge the fact that what Leslie has envisioned and shaped into being with her own hands belongs to her.

Our Creator God makes clear throughout Scripture that we, and all the earth, belong to Him. From the beginning of time, we are claimed by God as His own possession:

"Whatever is under the whole heaven is mine" (Job 41:11).

"The earth is the Lord's and the fullness thereof" (Ps. 24:1).

"Fear not, for I have redeemed you; I have called you by name, you are mine" (Is. 43:1).

"They shall be mine, says the LORD of hosts, in the day when I make up my treasured possession" (Mal. 3:17).

We are created to belong. It is no surprise, then, that the world's troubadours—poets, musicians and artists who give visual and verbal expression to longings of the soul—find that some of their most popular works are the ones that express a desire for somewhere to belong and someone to belong to. In Scripture we find the answer to these longings, for in them we find both the place where we belong and the person to whom we belong to.

Scripture tells us that God Himself is the dwelling place where we belong and where we find rest. "The eternal God is your dwelling place, and underneath are the everlasting arms" (Deut. 33:27). "Lord, you have been our dwelling place in all generations," the psalmist declares (Ps. 90:1) and "He who dwells in the shelter of the Most High will abide in the shadow of the Almighty" (91:1). We are "at home where we belong" when we live connected to the One who made us.

Christian mystics throughout the centuries have written of the soul's search for the place where it can rest. The most well-known words from early church leaders on the subject of the soul's belonging are those of Augustine, a fourth-century leader of the church. Augustine wrote some of the most quoted words in the history of the church: "Thou hast made us for Thyself, O God, and we are restless till we find rest in Thee."[2] In the early twentieth century, Indian missionary Sundar Singh wrote, "In comparison with this big world, the human heart is only a small thing. Though the world is so large, it is utterly unable to satisfy this tiny heart. The ever-growing soul and its capacity can be satisfied only in the infinite God. As water is restless until it reaches its level, so the soul has no peace until it rests in God."[3]

Much later in the same century, a young Turkish woman was baptized into new life as a Christian. She spoke these poignant words on her baptism day: "I came from a home without the love of my parents and, as a result of that, was always looking for love outside of my family, which only led to more hurt and pain. One day I saw a vision with a blackboard in it and the words, 'You belong to me. You are my girl.' Though I didn't understand the words then, I took comfort in them and decided I needed to find out whose girl I was." A young woman's search for identity and love ended when she discovered that she belonged to a Father in heaven who claimed and sought her for His own.

There is no getting around it: belonging is what we are made for. Created for God, we are lost apart from Him and restless until we find Him and return home to the dwelling place of our souls.

Robert McGee, author of *The Search for Significance*, frames the search in familiar psychological terms to show how restlessness can lead us away from a Designer-God connection rather than towards it:

From life's outset, we find ourselves on the prowl, searching to satisfy some inner, unexplained yearning. Our hunger causes us to search for people who will love us. Our desire for acceptance pressures us to perform to gain praise from others. We strive for success, driving our minds and bodies harder and further, hoping that because of our sweat and sacrifice others will appreciate us more. But the man or woman who lives only for the love and attention of others is never satisfied—at least, not for long. Despite our efforts, we will never find lasting, fulfilling peace if we must continually prove ourselves to others. Our desire to be loved and accepted is a symptom of a deeper need—the need that frequently governs our behavior and is the primary source of our emotional pain. Often unrecognized, this is our need for self-worth.[4]

God knows both the worth and the deep needs of the soul He created. "Deep calls to deep," He says to us in His Word (Ps. 42:7). In life with God, we find our worth secured and the longings of our heart fulfilled. Instead of pushing ourselves harder and further for acceptance, we rest in the truth that we are accepted already by someone. We have a place where we belong and where our natural and understandable needs for significance, security and satisfaction are met. The depths of God's creator heart calls to the deep longings of our created soul. *Be who you are meant to be— most fully alive, most deeply satisfied, most complete and most at rest when connected to the One who made you.*

Passion and commitment

The Bible makes another thing clear: the God who made us for Himself is both passionate about us and committed to being with us. Passion and commitment—we are attracted to these qualities and to the people who have them. We respect people who not only *say* they care about something but *show* they care by the way they live. This marriage of our words and our actions is called integrity and, we especially desire integrity in relationships. Who in the world does not want to hear "I am committed to you" and to see that these words are really true?

However, these words can sound too good to be true especially if we have heard them spoken but not often seen them in action. Yet, they are reassuringly credible from someone who has given the most convincing proof of His passion and whose commitment to us, in the words of Amy Carmichael, "cost Him blood."[5] We give ourselves to God in gratitude for what He has done for us, but He gave Himself to us for no other reason than love. We live life with God because we understand that we are most complete in this relationship, but God is complete in Himself and has no need of us for personal satisfaction, security, or significance.

God *chooses* life with us. This is an amazing truth. You and I are not needed by God. We have nothing to offer Him but "brokenness and strife," as the song goes.[6] Yet He welcomes us into His dwelling place and chooses to be with us.

God declares His love openly and without inhibition. "I have loved you with an everlasting love," He declares to Israel and to us through the prophet Jeremiah (31:3). "You are precious in my eyes, and honored, and I love you," He tells us through the prophet Isaiah (43:4). The Hebrew word translated "love" in both of these declarations is *ahab*, which signifies a love flowing from desire and delight.[7] This is the word used by a lover. It implies a focused and affectionate heart. Both passion and tenderness are captured in *ahab*, and by using this word to describe His love, God declares His heart as a lover and lays it before us.

The Hebrew word, *hesed*, describes another type of love that God feels for us. *Hesed* and its derivatives describe God's merciful love, His loving kindness and faithfulness.[8] "You have led in your steadfast love the people whom you have redeemed" (Exod. 15:13), Moses and the Israelites sing to the Lord after He brought them out of Egypt. "The Lord is faithful in all his words and kind in all his works," sings the psalmist (Ps. 145:13). "The steadfast love of the Lord never ceases; his mercies never come to an end" (Lam. 3:22).

Can we believe this kind of love and commitment? Can we take God at His Word and believe that whenever He thinks of us, there is desire and delight in His heart? That whenever He looks on us, there is faithfulness, kindness and mercy in His eyes? More often than not, we find it easier to tell others that God thinks this way about them than to believe it for ourselves. We know what we read in the Bible. We know what we are supposed to believe, but we also know how we are. And how can God really love us when he knows how we are?

A.W. Tozer wrote in *The Knowledge of the Holy*, "We are sure that there is in us nothing that could attract the love of One as holy and as just as Thou art . . . Yet," as he goes on to write in a prayer:

> Thou hast declared Thine unchanging love for us in Christ Jesus. If nothing in us can win Thy love, nothing in the universe can prevent Thee from loving us. Thy love is uncaused and undeserved. Thou art Thyself the reason for the love wherewith we are loved. Help us to believe the intensity, the eternity of the love that has found us. Then love will cast out fear; and our troubled hearts will be at peace, trusting not in what we are but in what Thou has declared Thyself to be.[9]

Can I read the words found in the Song of Solomon—"I am my beloved's, and his desire is for me" (7:10)—and believe they are true, not just for someone else but for me? When I not only read but believe these words, I find my deepest place of significance and my deepest place of rest.

"If you leave, I'm going with you"

In our early years of marriage, Louis and I lived in Co-
lumbia, South Carolina, in a rented house on a street called
Dinwood Circle. The street, true to its name, was more
than a cul-de-sac. Homes lined both sides of the street as
it wound its circular way off the main road and then back
again to the same point. Rarely did anyone drive through
Dinwood Circle unless you lived there or had lost your way.
It was a neighborhood in the truest sense of the word. Everyone knew each other's names, and someone was sure to be
working in their yard with time to chat as we walked around
"the circle" in the evening—which we did quite often. Most
of our neighbors were older couples who had lived there
for years. Louis and I gleaned quite a bit of wisdom during
those evening walks.

One evening, we were chatting by the mailbox with
a couple who lived next door and in the course of the
conversation learned that they had been married for nearly
thirty years. As we were soon to celebrate our third year of
marriage, this was an achievement that seemed wonderful
in our eyes. We asked them the secret of staying together
for so long. The husband looked at his wife with a twinkle
in his eyes and said, "I just told her early on that if she ever
leaves, I'm going with her." We laughed with him, but never
forgot his words. They have remained with us throughout
our now thirty plus years of marriage. Underneath the
humor was a serious commitment to relationship.

God says the same to us: "Just remember; when you
leave, I'm going with you." No one is more serious than God
about being with us. He declares this time and again to His
people:

To Isaac: "Sojourn in this land, and *I will be with you* and will bless you" (Gen. 26:3).

To Jacob: "*I myself will go down with you* to Egypt" (46:4).

To Moses: "*My presence will go with you*, and I will give you rest" (Exod. 33:14).

To Joshua: "Be strong and courageous. Do not be frightened, and do not be dismayed, for *the LORD your God is with you wherever you go*" (Josh. 1:9).

To Gideon: "But *I will be with you*, and you shall strike the Midianites as one man" (Judg. 6:16).

To the people of Israel through Isaiah: "When you pass through the waters, *I will be with you. . . . Fear not, for I am with you*" (Isa. 43:2, 5).

To Jeremiah: "Do not be afraid of them, for *I am with you* to deliver you" (Jer. 1:8).

None of these conversations were held in a place of worship. Each one took place in the nitty-gritty of life. Isaac was worried about his family's survival in a time of economic crisis; Jacob was on the verge of a major move; Moses was dealing with intense ministry pressures; Joshua faced a huge military campaign; Gideon felt inadequate to do what God was asking him to do, and Jeremiah faced hostility, slander and public humiliation from declaring the truth. In each case, God reminded them that they were not alone.

A dear friend of ours, Jim, is a retired seminary professor. When Louis was visiting Jim one day, Jim pulled out his Bible and read from Hebrews, "He [God] has said, 'I will never leave you nor forsake you'" (13:5). Jim explained to Louis how each time "never" in the English translation, it is a combination of two Greek negatives, *ou* and *me*. Put together, they form the strongest possible negative in the Greek language. Some Bible scholars suggest that an additional emphasis is implied due to the use of a structure equivalent to our English "neither . . . nor." Their equivalent today would be as forceful as saying, "No! Absolutely not! Don't even think of it! End of discussion."

Essentially, God says to us, "I will not, I will not, no, I will not, I will not leave you, nor will I forsake you." With a shake of his head, Jim leaned toward Louis and asked, "Now what about this promise do we not understand?"

One of God's names found in the Old Testament is Jehovah-Shammah,[10] which means "the LORD is there." Among the Old Testament prophecies is recorded another of His names: "She will give birth to a son and will call him Immanuel (which means 'God is with us')" (Isa. 7:14, NLT). The name and the prophecy re-emerge at the birth of Jesus (see Matt. 1:23). The fulfillment of the name "Immanuel" through Jesus is God's ultimate declaration of His commitment to be with us. His love is not only passionate, but pursuing. Jesus' death on the cross proved God's commitment to bring us home to where we belong. His resurrected life is a seal on the promise, "I am with you always, even to the end of the age" (28:20).

Our deepest significance

God has bestowed on us a great gift which brings deep rest to the soul. In our belonging to Him, God bestows on us the creation gift of significance. Significance comes from the meaning and value we place on something. We say a discovery is significant or someone makes a significant point because of the value we place on the new discovery or on the point which clarifies everything in a discussion. The watch I have worn for years has both meaning and value for me. It has personal significance because it is a gift from my daughter, and I value it more than a watch I would have bought for myself in a store.

God has given us both meaning and value from the beginning of time. Every baby—from the point of conception—is a new soul created for eternity with God. Our significance in the world rests in our significance for eternity. We are not merely physical bodies created to last for a limited number of years and at some point cease to exist. We are God-designed and God-breathed souls created for an eternal life with the One who bestowed on us life, value and meaning.

Once again, do we believe this? Once again, not so easily. Robert McGee notes that "Since the Fall, man has often failed to turn to God for the truth about himself. Instead, he has looked to others to meet his inescapable need for self-worth."[11] It is hard to believe that we are loved and valued to such a degree. It is hard to accept that we have a place of significance, already bestowed and readily available, if we will only return to it. We are often like the voice of longing and doubt expressed in a poem by Amy Carmichael:

> I thought I heard my Saviour say to me:
> 'My love will never weary, child, of thee.'
> Then in me, whispering doubtfully and low:
> How can that be?
> He answered me,
> 'But if it were not so,
> I would have told thee.'[12]

We are made to belong to God. We know this is true, because He has told us so. The One to whom we belong loves us passionately and is determined to be with us. This, too, He has told us. God does not look upon us with indifference, but rather as a lover who pursues the beloved, despite all imperfections, with passion and commitment. Like the young woman from Turkey who rested from her search for love when she found the lover of her soul, our souls find rest in the One who has created us for life with Him. Belonging to God and being loved by Him is our true significance in this world. No matter what life itself throws our way, we can rest because we know there is more in this world than meets the eye. There is life with God, love beyond measure and belonging for eternity.

Real Life with a Real God

"How few of us know that we are not our own and that we actually do belong to God! We have heard of it and read of it often and have perhaps thought we believed it; but really knowing it is a different matter. It is essential to our peace and well-being that we do know that we belong to God." –Hannah Whitall Smith[13]

1. What is your deepest "I am" at this time? Write a list of all the identities you have at this time. "I am a woman, man, sister, brother, husband, wife, parent, daughter, son, boss secretary, accountant, teacher . . ." These are true identities, and they shape who you are. At the same time, you are more than any of these. Write down the "I am . . ." identities which you have learned in this chapter.

2. Read Isaiah 43:1–13 to find answers to these questions:

   - Who am I?
   - Who is God?
   - What has God done for me?
   - What does He promise me?
   - What is my God-designed purpose?

3. As you read God's declarations of love and commitment in Isaiah 43, what is your initial response? Which truth, if any, do you find difficult to believe at this point in your life?

4. Talk with God about your feelings and doubts. If you have seen evidence of these truths in your life, thank Him. If you are still waiting to see evidence, talk with Him honestly about how you feel as you wait. God knows all that is in the heart and mind, so we can be completely honest with Him about what we feel and think.

2

Designed to Believe

To be trusted is a greater compliment than to be loved.
—George MacDonald[1]

Then God said . . . and it was so. (Gen. 1:29, 30)

I was recently having coffee with a young woman I have gotten to know since moving to Singapore. Gillian and I get together every few months, each time trying a new café for the rendezvous. This time it was my choice to find a place to meet. After an online search for the best coffee shops in Singapore, and there are many which claim this distinction, we met at the Chye Seng Huat Hardware. Despite the images evoked by such a name, it is one of Singapore's flagship coffee shops, boasting a roaster, coffee bar and a coffee school. Gillian and I were there, however, only for coffee and conversation, and both were enjoyed in abundance.

Much of the conversation on this day centered on the subject of marriage since Gillian is soon to enjoy that stage of life. But we also discussed life with God, and on this day we were talking about prayer. Gillian was wondering about the necessity of praying about everything, in this case her choice of a wedding dress as she was feeling somewhat guilty for not thinking much about God when she was trying on dresses. I suggested a more relaxed way of thinking about prayer; a way that sees prayer as bringing God's presence into the details of her life rather than about making sure she gets prayer and for that matter, everything else in life, perfectly right.

I was encouraging Gillian to think of prayer not as a duty of the Christian life but rather as a conversation with God. The idea of prayer as a God-connection in everything we do moves prayer from the realm of maintaining a ritual to that of maintaining a relationship—from a source of guilt (whether I am praying enough) to a source of delight (how I talk with God). Praying about her wedding dress is not so much about making the right choice on a dress but about enjoying God's presence in everything we do.

At this point Gillian made a comment that seemed unrelated to the topic, but was in fact, as I reflected on it later, directly connected.

"You and Louis seem so restful all the time," she said.

I must have looked confused, because quite honestly I was for the moment. Knowing the life we lead, I wondered how it could ever seem restful to others. But then, Gillian was not talking about the life we lead, which, truth be told, can be quite busy, but rather how she perceives we live in the midst of it. She went on to comment that no matter how busy we are, she has noticed that when we are with other people, as I was with her on this day, we seem relaxed. Not in a rush. Not making life all about *doing*. How can this be, she wondered?

All I can say is that Gillian does not live with us around the clock. Anyone, I imagine, can manage to look relaxed when drinking an exquisite cup of coffee while chatting with a friend in a flagship coffee bar, especially if that friend does not see you on a daily basis. Nonetheless, there was truth in Gillian's words in that life with God has shaped the way Louis and I think about work as the years go by. Intentional efforts to create space in our lives, space for rest and space for God, have been invaluable in maintaining perspective and balance.

There is a deeper reason, however, for possessing rest, no matter what runs riot in the world; a reason not explained by a balanced schedule, or anything else which is tied to the surface of life. This rest is explained only by something that lies under the surface and is so deeply planted that it is in the very core of our being. Everything flows from this central place of rest. The way we view the world, our circumstances, ourselves and—eventually, as we learn to live from this place of rest, even the way we handle the busyness of life—all are shaped by this inner place of rest which God has designed for the soul. We are created for significance, but we are also created for security, and God has given us a place where we are secure. Our deepest significance is in belonging to God and knowing His love for us. Our deepest security is in believing God and trusting His Word to us.

Our deepest security

Life happens and sometimes it hurts. Sometimes it confuses and disappoints. Sometimes it presses in so strongly that we feel nearly crushed by its weight. Sometimes it rains on our carefully planned parades. But the soul that lives in its God-designed place of security is a soul at peace. "You keep him in perfect peace whose mind is stayed on you, because he trusts in you," the prophet

Isaiah says to God (Is. 26:3). The psalmist declares about God that "for a thousand generations he's been as good as his word" (Ps. 105:8, THE MESSAGE). In other words, God is true to His promises. He is as good as His Word. We can count on what He says.

Most of us know what it means to appreciate someone we can count on. Someone who fulfills his commitments and, to put it bluntly, does what he says he will do. Louis and I are blessed to know quite a few people who fit this description. Some of them form the team we currently work with in our mission's international office. The fact that this team is made up of people we enjoy being with is a plus since we spend a lot of time together, but what matters when it comes to work is not that we can laugh together but that we can count on each other.

Having such colleagues is a bonus to the work we do, but having someone we can count on for *everything* in life is a gift indeed; someone whose word we can trust and whose character we can rely on when life confuses, discourages or disappoints. Maybe you have never felt such confidence because there has been no one in your life who has told the truth or kept a promise. Maybe you have never met a person of real integrity, someone whose character is the same in public as it is in private. If so, you are in good company with the psalmist who complained about some of the people he knew: "For there is no truth in their mouth; their inmost self is destruction; their throat is an open grave; they flatter with their tongue" (5:9). The words are quite strong, but we have to admit that the same could be said of many people today. The Psalms, and all of the Bible for that matter, are about real life. Lack of integrity is all too real in the broken world in which we live, yet the world was founded on the integrity of a spoken word.

In the beginning

The power and integrity of God's spoken word are evident from the beginning. Throughout the Genesis account of creation two phrases are recorded repeatedly: *God said . . . and it was so. God said . . . and it was so. God said . . . and it was so.* When God speaks, things happen. What He declares is so. If anything exists in the world, it exists because God exists. If anything is true in the world, it is true because the One who made the world is true and He has declared truth to the world. The first chapter of Genesis is not only a record of creation but a reference for God's character. Truth did not begin with creation. It was already present in the One who spoke the world into existence.

The integrity of God's Word cannot be emphasized enough. Many people believe *in* God, yet do not *believe Him.* They acknowledge God exists but do not believe that what He says is necessarily true. The difference between believing in God and believing Him is significant. God's Word is His bond, as the saying goes. There is something to count on in the newly created world, and that is the Word of its Maker.

God is the source of "all things bright and beautiful," to quote a phrase from an old Anglican hymn. He is the source of life and "in him we live and move and have our being" (Acts 17:28). The way to live and move and have our being is found in trusting the word of the One who made us:

- *A word designed to protect:* "May your love and faithfulness always protect me" (Ps. 40:11, NIV).

- *A word designed to guide:* "Guide me in your truth and teach me, for you are God my Savior" (Ps. 25:5, NIV).

- *A word designed to strengthen:* "My soul melts away for sorrow; strengthen me according to your word!" (Ps. 119:28).

- *A word designed to set free:* "I will walk about in freedom, for I have sought out your precepts" (Ps. 119:45, NIV).

- *A word designed to give rest:* "Great peace have those who love your law; nothing can make them stumble" (Ps. 119:165).

God's Word, true and eternal, is given to the newly created soul as its deepest place of security. We are made to believe the One we belong to. By taking God at His Word, we gain confidence, we learn to rest and we learn how to live as we are meant to live. Francois Fénelon, a spiritual mentor to many in the seventeenth century, put it well in a letter to a struggling Christian: "Our confidence is neither in frail men nor in ourselves, as frail as others. Our confidence is in God only, the one unchanging Truth. Let all mankind prove themselves to be mere men—that is to say, nothing but falsehood and sin. Still God's truth will not be weakened."[2]

Taking God at His Word does not lead to an unrealistic view of the world we inhabit. The Bible is full of real people with real emotions and sometimes embarrassingly honest responses to life. If you are not sure of this, read the stories of Moses, Abraham, Gabriel, Hannah or Peter, to name just a few. Read Habakkuk's fiery dialogue with God. Spend time

in the Psalms. If God wanted us to have an unrealistic view
of life with Him, He would not have allowed such notori-
ously imperfect examples of "pillars of faith." Nor would He
have allowed such depths of anger, doubt, weariness, deception and depression to mingle with the declarations of praise
and faith found throughout the Bible.

God understands the deep places of the soul. Having
created us with emotions, He understands our emotions and
is certainly big enough to handle what emotions we throw
His way. The key is that, like the men and women of Scripture, we know where to go with our feelings. Whether we are
feeling anxiety, doubt, anger, confusion, depression or fear,
God is a secure place to go with all that we feel and think.
We speak to Him honestly about all that is in our hearts and
minds, and He speaks to us equally honestly from His heart
and mind which is revealed to us in His Word. Believing
God does not make us unrealistic about life. Instead, it gives
us a real hope in the midst of life.

"Now faith is the assurance of things hoped for, the con-
viction of things not seen" (Heb. 11:1).

"We look not to the things that are seen but to the things
that are unseen" (2 Cor. 4:18).

"'The LORD is my portion,' says my soul, 'therefore I will
hope in him.' The LORD is good to those who wait forhim,
to the soul who seeks him" (Lam. 3:24–25).

Real hope in the midst of real life

Two of my spiritual mentors from the past are Amy
Carmichael and Andrew Murray. Both wrote prolifically
and even today their books continue to draw readers into
a deeper life with God. Andrew Murray was already a well-

known speaker and writer on the spiritual life when Amy Carmichael was a young missionary recently home from Japan and recovering from burnout after her first years on the mission field. During her recovery period, she attended a conference where Murray was the speaker and had an opportunity to meet him in person. Murray's books had influenced her own walk with Christ, so when she was about to hear him speak, she wondered, "Was he as good as his books?"

They were housed in the same guest house during the conference, so Amy had plenty of opportunities to answer her question as she met Andrew Murray on a daily basis. After observing and interacting with him for the length of the conference, she wrote in her journal:

> Was he as good as his books? He was better; for there was not only goodness, there was a delicious dry humour, dauntless courage, and the gentleness and simplicity of a dear child. And he was very loving. He never seemed to be tired of loving. Then something painful happened. This is how he met it: he was quiet for a while with his Lord, then he wrote these words for himself:
>
> *First*, He brought me here; it is by His will that I am in this strait place; in that fact I will rest.
>
> *Next*, He will keep here in His love, and give me grace to behave as His child.
>
> *Then*, He will make the trial a blessing, teaching me the lessons He intends me to learn, and working in me the grace He means to bestow.
>
> *Last*, in His good time He can bring me out again—how and when He knows.
>
> Let me say I am here, (1) by God's appointment, (2)

in His keeping, (3) under His training, and (4) for His time.[3]

The young and weary missionary had an opportunity to observe closely a famous writer and speaker and found that he was even better than his books. She saw that he was true to the words he wrote when "real life" happened in a public place. Gentleness of character, courage, a sense of humor and a loving nature are easy to project when life goes well, but what happens when life goes wrong? She watched him take something painful to God and draw strength from Him. She saw him take God at His Word, no matter how real the pain of his circumstances.

Andrew Murray had learned that rest in the middle of painful circumstances comes from entrusting himself and his situation to God. We, too, can have this rest. When life's reality hits hard and comes fast, we can find that our security is not in changing circumstances but in an unchanging God.

A more modern, and perhaps easier to relate to, example of real hope in the midst of real life is the story of Richard and Geneva Culp.[4] The Culps owned a farm in California and worked hard to keep it going, but eventually, life brought not just one but a series of challenging circumstances. One after another, they were hit hard by situations beyond their control and although they worked faithfully to keep the farm going, the time came when they not only lost the farm but were left with a huge debt. Even so, Richard said, "In spite of the overwhelming grief and loss, I knew that God was in control of our situation. I remembered the Bible story of Joseph. Even as a slave and prisoner, that young man was part of God's glorious plan. As for me, I knew that God must have something better for our future, too."

The Culps had a strong trust in God, but things did not improve. In fact, they became worse. Richard had another job apart from their farm but soon lost that job. They had to move into rental housing and look for minimum wage jobs to pay the bills and clear their debt. Finally, a steady job did come through, and they were able once again to have steady income. After working the new job for a year, the Culps received a phone call from the head of the credit company who had taken away their farm. He wanted to talk with them and was even willing to drive out to the club for the conversation. The Culps agreed, and they met together at the club. After talking about various things, eventually the company head came to his real reason for seeking them out. A personal friend had recently lost everything he owned and the friend's wife had committed suicide. At the office, people remembered the Culps' situation and were aware of how differently the two couples had responded to a similar crisis. They were wondering, quite honestly, what was the Culps' secret.

Richard had an opportunity to explain their source of hope and he did so without hesitation because it was based on something the couple had settled in their minds even before the financial storm hit. "We believe in the God of the Bible," he told the company head. "He is sovereign over our lives, and he is in control. Even though the pain is real, we are confident of this: God has proven sufficient and able to take care of us."

The Culps' deepest place of security was not in visible things but in things invisible to the eye. Their deepest place of security was God and their deepest "I believe" was His Word. The Hebrew word for believe is *aman*. It carries the weight of an exhortation to be firm, to stand still or to be settled.[5] It calls to mind the parable of Jesus about a man who builds his house on a rock rather than on sand: "Everyone then who hears these words of mine and does them will be like a wise man who built his house on the rock. And the rain fell, and the floods came, and the winds blew and beat on that house, but it did not fall, because it had been founded on the rock." (Matt. 7:24–25). The Culps are a modern-day example of this parable. Their life was built on God's Word, and their minds settled on His promises, so when the storm hit, they were able to stand.

"Already settled." These are firm words. Final words. Restful words. They are words that have authority. If something is already settled, there is nothing to be done but accept it. Louis and I recently went out to dinner for a Friday night date. As we entered the restaurant of choice for the evening, we saw a friend sitting at a table with a group of people and went over to greet her. After a few minutes of conversation, we sat down at our own table and enjoyed our meal, only pausing to say goodbye to our friend when the group left after about an hour. A little later we were ready to leave and asked the waiter for the bill. "No need," she said, "your bill is already settled." Our friend had paid our bill on her way out! All was done. A debt was paid. There was nothing more we needed to do or even could do but leave with full stomachs and a thankful heart.

What is "already settled" in your mind? Is your mind settled on God's Word? Yes, there is what you see happening around you. These are very real circumstances which are, quite frankly, worrisome and confusing and even frightening. There is very real pain. But to the one who is "already settled" on God's Word, there is also very real hope and rest. Another reality is at work, unseen with the physical eyes but seen clearly with the eyes of faith, and that is God's reality which is backed by His Word.

One of the most important questions we will ever answer is the question, "Am I settled on God's Word?" And how do we become settled on His Word rather than on the other words that enter our minds through the myriad of voices we hear every day—the voices of media, of other people, of our own thoughts and feelings which are not grounded on truth? We listen to God speak through His Word as much, and in fact more, than we listen to the other voices which speak into our lives.

Dietrich Bonhoeffer gives us good advice through his classic work on the church, *Life Together*:

> "The Word of Scripture should never stop sounding in your ears and working in you all day long, just like the words of someone you love. And just as you do not analyze the words of someone you love, but accept them as they are said to you, accept the Word of Scripture and ponder it in your heart, as Mary did. That is all. . . . Do not ask, 'How shall I pass it on?' but 'What does it say to me?' Then ponder this word long in your heart until it has gone right into you and taken possession of you."[6]

Do we believe God? Do we take Him at His Word? Are we listening to God speak as much as we are listening to others? Our answers to these questions will determine everything we do. It will determine how we view our circumstances and respond to them, how we feel about ourselves, how we relate to the people around us, how we live and how we die. It will mean the difference between a life shaped by anxiety and one shaped by rest. We are made to believe and to live from this God-designed place of security. Our soul's built-in security system is the integrity of God and the truth of His Word. If, when the storms come, we are already settled in our minds that we take God at His word, we will not be shaken.

Real Life with a Real God

"Lord, your best servants are those who wish to shape their life on your answers rather than shape your answers on their wishes."–Augustine[7]

1. Time for honest reflection: What is your deepest "I believe?" To help in this reflection, consider what you often think or verbalize to others about yourself. What you are thinking and saying about a current situation you are facing?

2. Write a list of "I believe that I am ___" statements followed by "I believe God is ___." If the statements are biblically based, such as "I believe I am loved by God" or "I believe God is in control," then ask yourself, "Do I really believe this?" Does it reflect in the way I think and speak? In the way I respond to other people and to circumstances?

3. Reflect on this past week by asking the following questions:

   • What are ways I have acted or reacted which reveal that I am not resting in God's Word?

   • What are ways I have acted or reacted which reveal that I am not resting in God's love, either for myself or for someone I am concerned about?

4. What influences me most in the way I think about God, about myself, or about the circumstances I am currently facing?

    •   The opinions of other people?
    •   What I watch on television or read on the Internet?
    •   What I see in the mirror (physically or emotionally)?
    •   What I read in God's Word?

5. Isaiah 43:10 says that we are chosen to "know Him and believe Him." We often talk of the difference between knowing about God and knowing Him personally. What is the difference between believing in God and believing Him?

6. Read Luke 4:1–13, noting the temptations that Jesus faced and how He met them.

7. Read Psalm 27 as a conversation with God. He is speaking to you through His Word and you are responding in prayer:

    •   What situations come to mind as you read through the Psalm?
    •   What people come to mind?
    •   What is God saying about your life with Him?
    •   Whenever a situation or person or area of conviction comes to mind, stop reading and talk with God. Use words from the Psalm as you pray. Then continue reading and listening to God through His Word.

3

Designed to Be Image-Bearers

To make us in His own image is the object
of God's workmanship and nothing short of this will accomplish
His divine purpose in our creation.
–Hannah Whitall Smith[1]

When God created man, he made him in the
likeness of God. (Gen. 5:1)

Significance and security are gifts from God to each one of us. We did nothing to earn them, and they are ours through nothing of our own making. To live in our God-designed place of significance and place of security is to be the real you, the real me. Yet, as good as it is to be significant and secure, there is more to life than feeling good about ourselves and being confident in what we believe. There is something called purpose which takes us outside of ourselves and gives meaning to our lives in a larger context. Discovering this purpose and living by it leads us to our soul's deepest place of satisfaction.

When we go to the Bible, the operating manual of the world, we learn a startling thing. You and I are designed for glory. Not ours, of course, but God's. Built into our system is the ability to reflect the wonder and glory of the God who made us. It should be automatic; not something we do by effort, but rather something we cannot help but do, simply because this is who we are. God planted such a possibility in us at creation, and He chose, for some reason, to give this possibility only to humans. The animals, insects, reptiles and plants of the world are amazing, but the human creation is even more so. God's plan from the beginning was that humans alone are to reflect His likeness in the world.

Then God said, "Let us make man in our image, after our likeness. . . .so God created man in his own image, in the image of God he created him, male and female he created them" (Gen. 1:26–27).

The Hebrew word translated in Genesis as "likeness" comes from a verb which means "to compare." The word itself, *demuth*, can be translated "likeness, resemblance; image, model, pattern, or shape."[2] "Let us make man," God says in effect, "to resemble us, to be modeled after us. When others compare them with us, there will be a likeness. They will be able to say, 'Yes, I can see the family resemblance.'"

As I write, Father's Day is approaching, which brings to mind the men in my family. Our son, Scott, bears a resemblance to both Louis's and my side of the family. He looks like his maternal grandfather—so much so that when people see a portrait of my father and then see Scott, they do a double take. The appearance of my father as a younger man and my son as a young adult is so striking that Scott often hears the remark, "We can tell where you come from!"

Scott looks like his grandfather, but he sounds like his father. He has Louis's unmistakable deep voice. It is the kind of voice that makes people say, "You should be a radio announcer." During our last six years of missionary service in

Chad, Scott and his sisters attended a boarding school in Germany. They would return to Chad during the Christmas and summer vacations, but once a year we flew to them and spent two weeks of their spring break together in Europe. On one of these annual visits to Germany, Louis phoned the house where Scott lived so he would know we had arrived in town. Another student answered the phone, and Louis asked to speak to Scott. "Cut it out, Scott," the student said. "I know it's you." It took some time for Louis to convince the student that he was speaking to the father and not the son. Needless to say, the young man apologized profusely and ran to find Scott as quickly as he could!

More recently, I was talking with my daughter, Elisabeth, and heard her use a phrase I have said for many years. It startled me to hear her say it so unconsciously, and I thought, *That's me!* I kept the revelation to myself to spare Elisabeth the pain of discovering that at twenty-two she was already sounding like her mother, but I couldn't help smiling as I thought about it later. My daughter has heard me speak certain words over and over throughout her life. They now come naturally from her own lips.

We are designed to bear a similar family likeness. From the very first God-breathed souls on earth, humans were intended to belong to God, to believe Him and to bear His image by reflecting His character and His words in the world. When people look at us, they should see the resemblance. They should notice a likeness to the One who made us—not an external, physical likeness, of course, but an internal likeness of spirit and of character. When we speak, we should sound increasingly like our heavenly Father as our words reflect things we have heard Him say to us throughout the years. Fulfilling this God-designed purpose of image-bearing is our deepest satisfaction, because we are who we are meant to be.

From the very beginning, our wholeness as human beings was linked to the image of God. But how are we meant to live as we bear His likeness? We have already seen that love—passionate, committed and merciful—is at the core of God's character. So is truth. God is not just loving in what He does and truthful in what He says, He is love and He is truth. He can be no other way. To bear the family likeness is to be loving and truthful and to be able to act in no other way. But what else was put into the soul naturally made for image-bearing? When we see God in His Word, we see that He is loving, merciful, faithful and truthful, but also relational, holy and righteous, a lover of diversity, caring for His creation and life-giving in all He does.

God is relational

Those familiar with the mystery of a Triune God understand that God Himself exists in relationship. Psychologist and author, Larry Crabb has said that the Father, Son and Holy Spirit is the only small group in existence that works perfectly. His words may draw a laugh, as they are intended to do, but Crabb is perfectly serious and his theology is correct. God exists in relationship and has also designed us to live in relationship. Kenneth Boa writes in *Conformed to His Image:* "Because God is a relational being, the two great commandments of loving him and expressing this love for him by loving others are also intensely relational. We were created for fellowship and intimacy not only with God but also with each other."[3]

Relationships are some of our greatest sources of joy, but they can also be the source of some of our greatest challenges. "I love my job," we hear people say, and they sometimes add, "but it's the people that bother me." Relationships, even our closest ones, bring some of our greatest challenges in life. It was not meant to be this way, but then, we are not living as we are meant to live. The real you is designed to live in a harmonious connection with the world and with each other. God's relational image in us, along with other aspects of His character, guaranteed this. Instead, we are disconnected from God and live in a broken world. We rub shoulders with its brokenness every day, and this includes a brokenness in our relationships.

Kenneth Boa reminds us that our connection with God and our connection with others are really two sides of a single coin: "Loving God completely is the key to loving self correctly (seeing ourselves as God sees us) and this in turn is the key to loving others compassionately."[4] Only in a right connection with God are we able to live as we are meant to live, in right relationships with each other.

God is holy and righteous

When you read the words *holy* and *righteous*, does your mind grow numb? Do you think "been there, heard that" and, to be honest, prefer not to hear so much about it now? What about the word "justice"? Now there's a word we can use more easily. Involvement with issues of justice is a necessary labor in today's world but also are a true reflection of God's righteousness. He makes it very clear in Scripture that heartfelt participation in works of justice and mercy are more acceptable to Him than superficial behaviors of fasting and sacrifice in the temple (see Isa. 58:6–12).

God's righteousness moves us to work for justice, and we bear His image when we do so. We encounter a problem, however, when we proclaim God's call to live justly and work for justice but leave behind His equal call for holiness. God is equally clear that we are to be holy as He is holy (see Lev. 11:44–45; 19:2; Eph. 1:4). There is a right and a wrong way to live, but to suggest so is not politically correct in today's world. God's justice is in vogue, but His holiness is out of fashion, even sometimes in the church.

"There was a time," writes renowned theologian J.I. Packer in *Rediscovering Holiness*, "when all Christians laid great emphasis on God's call to holiness. But how different it is today! To listen to our sermons and to read the books we write, and then to watch the zany, worldly, quarrelsome way we behave, you would never imagine that once the highway of holiness was clearly marked out for Bible-believers."[5]

Perhaps there is a reason for a growing aversion to mentioning God's holiness in public places. A focus on holiness conjures up images of some Christian voices which we prefer not to be associated with. We do not want to be seen as dogmatic, narrow-minded or intolerant and so avoid any vocabulary associated with these voices. Or perhaps the aversion stems more from how we choose to live. A mention of God's holiness makes us uncomfortable because it demands something that we ourselves are not willing to do. Yes, God has declared there is a way for His people to live, but we prefer to live another way and, to be honest, we prefer a God who lets us. To meet this personal and sometimes congregational dilemma, we are tempted to do one of two things. We either reduce God's expectation of holiness in order to justify our choices or diminish His call to be holy and elevate His call to love. Yet, to be our true selves, we must include both holiness and love in the way we live. The problem is often not a view of holiness that is too low but rather a view of God that does not reach high enough.

We are "created after the likeness of God in true righteousness and holiness" (Eph. 4:24). We often associate holiness and righteousness with behavior, but Scripture includes the way we think as well as the way we act. Behavior, in God's mind, merely reflects what is in the heart. When God calls us to be holy as He is holy, He calls us to wholeness of life. A God-designed holiness has less to do with an image we might project on the outside, and everything to do with what God sees within.

Jesus taught that "what comes out of the mouth proceeds from the heart, and this defiles a person. For out of the heart come evil thoughts, murder, adultery, sexual immorality, theft, false witness, slander" (Matt. 15:18–19). Sadly, His words to the religious leaders can be equally true for us today: "You also outwardly appear righteous to others, but within you are full of hypocrisy and lawlessness" (23:28). Jesus fully understood that holiness is a high standard. He fully understood that as we pursue holiness we need much grace (the cross is evidence of this), but He also understood that the holiness God proclaimed to His people had become reduced to outward behavior and cultural patterns. The same could be said of the church today, as Jerry Bridges writes:

"Many Christians have what we might call a 'cultural holiness.' They adapt to the character and behavior pattern of Christians around them. As the Christian culture around them is more or less holy, so these Christians are more or less holy. But God has not called us to be like those around us. He has called us to be like himself. Holiness is nothing less than conformity to the character of God."[6]

What does it mean for us to live holy lives? J. C. Ryle defines holiness as "the habit of being of one mind with God. . . . It is the habit of agreeing in God's judgment, hating what He hates, loving what He loves, and measuring everything in this world by the standard of His Word."[7]

What does holiness look like? It looks like Jesus, who is holiness in human form. J. I. Packer sums it up this way: "And what is human godliness, the godliness that is true holiness, as seen in Jesus? It is simply human life lived as the Creator intended . . . an existence in which the elements of the human person are completely united in a totally God-honoring and nature-fulfilling way."[8]

God loves diversity

One only has to look out the window to see that variety in the plant and animal world was in the plan for creation, and not just a limited variety, either. The number of species of beetles alone is over one million. The mind boggles at such a thought. But beyond the amazing diversity in nature is the diversity within the human race. Flowing from God's love of diversity is the range of physical features, personalities, gifts and abilities we see in humans. Louis and I are privileged to travel quite a bit in our ministry, and I am constantly amazed by the physical diversity that is evident from Mexico to Russia to Chad to India to Korea. Then there is the diversity which is not immediately obvious but which becomes evident when we spend time together with other people. Some of us are introverts and others are extroverts; some see the big picture when considering a new idea and others see the details; some prefer the samba and others prefer ballet; some love to worship with exuberant music and others prefer quiet liturgies and traditional hymns. We are not all the same in personality, gifts, personal interests or even in our preferred ways of drawing near to God—nor are we meant to be. To bear the family likeness does not mean that we each look and act the same. It does mean that whatever personalities we have, whatever gifts and abilities, whatever personal preferences for music or literature or vocation, we are at our best when these are shaped by the One who made us.

I can still remember sitting in the stadium of the University of North Carolina waiting for our daughters' graduation ceremony to begin. Like the majority of the waiting crowd, I spent the initial minutes reading through the program we were handed as we entered the stadium. After locating Susan's and Elisabeth's names in the program and trying unsuccessfully to find their faces in the student section of the stadium, I turned my attention to the masters and doctoral degrees listed in the program. A superficial scan of names soon became an absorbed fascination with the variety of subjects chosen for dissertations. I was amazed that someone had spent countless hours of his life researching the foraging behavior of the predatory mite or the salivary glands of the pea aphid. And yet, why not? The world is an amazing and diverse place and so are the people who find interest in it. Our personalities and interests, along with the natural gifts and surrounding cultures that shape us, are part of our uniquely God-designed selves.

We tend to file the plethora of data of physical, intellectual, relational, cultural and vocational differences in scientific folders, relegating our vast diversity as human beings to physical origins. Yet, the diversity we see so clearly just by looking around us is directly related to our God-designed purpose and satisfaction as image-bearers. "For you formed my inward parts," the psalmist declares to God. "I praise you, for I am fearfully and wonderfully made. Wonderful are your works; my soul knows it very well" (Ps. 139:13–14).

All the varied ways in which we live in the world—whether we prefer the beach or the mountains for vacation, choose to play tennis or read a book on a day off, dance the samba or the waltz, study pea aphids or create jewelry, love a party or prefer quiet conversations over coffee, draw nearer to God through exuberant worship or through the quiet words of liturgy, become an accountant or a counselor, care for the elderly or care for the earth, work for justice or teach literacy—all flow from a Designer God and are meant to reflect something of who He is in the world He created.

To bear God's likeness does not eliminate uniqueness as individuals. A diamond shines more brilliantly with many facets than with one flat surface. In the same way, our diversity reflects the fullness of God's glory.

God cares for the created world

No matter what one may think of over-zealous and tunnel-visioned conservationists, we are to care for the earth we inhabit. The earth's resources are indeed limited, and that is a valid reason to care, but as Christians we care for a deeper reason. We care because God cares for the earth He brought into existence. As Christians, we have on our hearts what is on the heart of God, and the fact that God loves all of His creation, not just humans, is seen clearly in the creation account.

We sense God's delight in His creation as He gives the command to multiply in numbers. *Let's have more of the same! It's really good!* We see His concern for the created world when He commands Adam to take care of it (see Gen. 1:28; 2:15). Four Hebrew words are used in the recorded accounts of God's command to Adam in relation to the earth and its creatures. In the first account God tells Adam to *kabash* (bring things under control, subdue)[9] and to *radah* (rule, reign).[10] One can only imagine what a riot of fauna and tangle of flora those early days must have been. You can almost hear God saying to Adam, "I love this mess and all these creatures, but left to itself the kudzu will take over and left to themselves the chimps will run riot; it would be good to have some order around here."

The creation account continues with two words that further emphasize God's love for all He created. He places Adam in the garden not only to rule but to *abad*, which carries dual meanings of "serve" and "work"[11] and to *samar* which means "to keep or guard."[12] Adam is put in charge of the created world, and his responsibilities are to be characterized by service and care. *I'm putting you in charge, Adam. Work the earth but also watch over it and care for it.*

One could reasonably think I am drawing too much from a few chapters at the beginning of the Bible, but God's concern for creation is evident beyond Genesis. When He gives the laws which are to govern Israel's life as a nation, God includes laws for animal protection (see Gen. 6:19;

Exod. 23:12; Deut. 25:4). Most interesting is His inclusion of care of the earth in the laws which govern Israel's Sabbath rest (Lev. 25:2–5). We are familiar with the Sabbath rhythm of six days of work and one day of rest for ourselves, but God considers that the earth labors as well and tells the people of Israel to let the land rest, not every seventh day but every seventh year.

Bearing the family likeness means that we, too, care for the earth we inhabit. Yes, we use the earth's resources for our existence but we nurture the earth for its own existence, not just for ours. It is true that we are spiritual beings, destined for eternity and living only momentarily in time, but while we are on earth, God intends for us to care for it.

God is life-giving

The whole of Scripture is a testimony to God's commitment to life. From the beginning when He "formed the man of dust from the ground and breathed into his nostrils the breath of life" (Gen. 2:7) to the end when there is the presence of a tree of life in John's vision of the end times (see Rev. 22:2), life is on God's mind, and He wants life for us. "Therefore choose life," He says to Israel and to us, "that you and your offspring may live loving the LORD your God, obeying his voice and holding fast to him, for he is your life" (Deut. 30:19–20).

An image of life runs throughout the Bible in the form of a river. A river in Genesis waters the garden which flows in Eden (see Gen. 2:6). In the Psalms, there is a river "whose streams make glad the city of God" (46:4). In Ezekiel's vision of the moment when God's glory returns to His people, a river begins to flow from the temple and increases in width and depth as it expands, bringing life wherever it flows (see Ezek. 47:8–9).

The river in Ezekiel's vision returns in John's vision of the heavenly throne: "Then the angel showed me the river of the water of life, bright as crystal, flowing from the throne of God and of the Lamb through the middle of the street of the city" (Rev. 22:1–2). In John's vision, a tree of life borders the river, a tree whose leaves are for the healing of the nations.

Ezekiel's vision and John's vision are of a life-giving river that flows from God's presence. Jesus refers to this same life-giving water when He extends an invitation to return to our place of security. Believing is connected with this image of life: "Whoever believes in me, as the Scripture has said, 'Out of his heart will flow rivers of living water'" (John 7:38).

It brings life wherever it goes. "Out of his heart will flow rivers of living water." What do you think when you read these words? I read them and something rises up from a deep place within me. I long for these words to be true in my own life. I long to be someone who brings life wherever she goes. To bring life and not death in the way I speak and the way I relate to people. To live as I am meant to live; but only a connection to God Himself, the source of life, will make this possible.

To be or not to be

God is loving, truthful and relational. He is holy, righteous and life-giving. He has a concern for all He has created and is delighted with its uniqueness. God can act in no other way, because these qualities are His very nature. The incredible thing is that He has given these qualities to us when He made us in His image. As image-bearers, they are as natural to us as they are to God. This is the real you and the real me. This is the way we are meant to live. This is where we find satisfaction.

Or, rather, this is how we are supposed to live. We don't need to read or hear the daily news of what's happening in the world to realize that something has gone terribly wrong. We only need to look within to see that we are not living as we are meant to live.

Do you remember my friend, Leslie, the creator of beautiful things? As she holds a new mound of clay in her hands, she envisions a serving dish or vase or coffee mug. Or maybe she has in mind something different, something which will have no other purpose than to sit on a shelf and be appreciated "as is." Truly, I believe she envisions and shapes each one out of love: a love for the creative process, a love for pottery in particular and a creator's love for each piece formed first in her mind and then through her hands.

Each piece has a purpose for which it was made and rightly belongs to Leslie. Unless, of course, she gives it away. I, for one, am thankful that Leslie is in the habit of doing so because she knows I love pottery and has given me several pieces of her work. Most recently, she gave me a sugar and creamer set, which I was delighted to receive.

I look at the pieces now in my kitchen beside our coffee maker. Because they bear Leslie's name, I will always know who created them. I also know what she had in mind when forming them, since they have the unmistakable shape of a sugar and creamer set. But they belong to me now and as their new owner, I could use them for something other than what Leslie intended. I could, for example, put a bouquet of short-stemmed flowers in the creamer pitcher and set it on the window sill to bask in the sun or put peanuts in the sugar bowl for the next time we have guests. Leslie might laugh if she notices a flower in a piece of pottery that she has made to hold cream or raise her eyebrows at the peanuts where sugar was supposed to be, but having given away her creations, she can no longer dictate how they will be used, no matter how far they have strayed from her intended purpose.

You and I are very much like the sugar bowl and creamer pitcher that now sit in my kitchen. We too were made for a purpose. We too are far from home. But there is a significant difference. Unlike Leslie's pottery, God never gave us away. Instead, we gave ourselves away. What happened in the beginning so soon after the world began is often called the Fall. When theologians write about the Fall or when pastors preach and teachers teach on it, they mean "the fall of mankind" or "humankind" as we are wont to say today. The use of the word "fall" implies an accident. One never means to fall but it happens. We trip on something or lose our balance and can't catch ourselves, so we fall. This much is true. Mankind did trip on some-thing—his own self. He stumbled and was not be able to catch himself. The Fall was real and so are its consequences in the world.

What happened in the garden was not an accident, how-ever. It was a choice; a choice which resulted in a transfer of trust and a shift of allegiance. Adam and Eve chose to hand over the soul's allegiance from its creator and greatest lover to its greatest enemy. This "Great Handover," as I have come to think of Adam and Eve's movement from life to death, led to the "Great Disconnect" of their souls, and consequently of every soul to be born after.

The real you, the real me, was lost at the Great Handover. We can no longer be with the One we belong to, and we can no longer bear His image. We have lost everything that enables us to live as we are meant to live. Understanding who we are meant to be, as we have seen in these first chapters, and understanding how we lost everything, as we will see in the next, is essential to understanding how life is made possible once again through Christ.

Real Life with a Real God:

"I would rather be what God chose to make me than the most glorious creature that I could think of; for to have been thought about, born in God's thought, and then made by God, is the dearest, grandest, and most precious thing in all thinking."–George MacDonald[13]

1. Time for more honest reflection. What is your deepest "I want"? Answering this question reveals where we are looking for satisfaction. Write a list of statements beginning "I want_____." Many of these are good desires, so don't feel bad about writing "I want health" or "I want a good marriage" or "a good job" or "for my children to know and honor Christ." Then reflect on a life without these desires being fulfilled. Would you be able to say "God is enough for me" or "His presence and His purpose are enough for me?"

2. Bring each of these desires before God, trusting Him to fulfill them according to His good and wise ways, but also putting them in their proper place. They are good and natural desires, but their fulfilment will not bring our deepest satisfaction.

3. Read Isaiah 43:7 and Ephesians 1:11–14.
   What do these verses say about our reason for existence?
   How does being an image-bearer help us fulfill our pur-
   pose? What do you think it means to bear the likeness of
   God?

4. What do 2 Corinthians 3:18 and Colossians 1:27 suggest about image-bearing?

5. The Bible is filled with references to who God is and
   how we are to live. The Scriptures are very deep waters
   indeed. What follows will only take us snorkeling when
   we really need to be scuba diving, but they give a beginning point for personal study on each aspect of God's
   nature.

   Holy and righteous:
   Ex. 20:8–11   Isa. 58:6–12
   Lev. 20:7–8, 26; 22:9   Luke 1:35, 46–55
   I Sam. 2:1–3   Eph. 1:4
   Ps. 24:3–6; 36:5–6   Col. 1:21–23
   Prov. 29:7   1 Pet. 1:13–15

   Life-giving:
   Deut. 4:39–40; 30:11–20   John 10:10; 17:6
   Ps. 16:11; 36:7–9   2 Pet. 1:3–4
   Rom. 6:22–23   1 John 1:24–25
   John 5:21, 24–26; 6:47–51, 57,   Rev. 21:22– 27
   66–69

   Loving diversity and creation:
   Rom. 1:18–25: note the difference between caring for
   creation and worshiping it.
   Gen. 1:11–12, 20–25   1 Cor. 12:4–11,
                                        27–31

Ps. 65:9–13; 104:24–26   Heb. 4:13

Rom. 8:19; 12:3–8   Rev. 7:9

Relational:

Ex. 20:1–17: note the "with-God" relational command-ments and the "with each other" relational command ments.

Ps. 133:1   Phil. 2:1–14

Rom. 12:9–21   Col. 3:9–14

4

The Great Handover

There are two ways to be fooled. One is to believe what isn't true;
the other is to refuse to believe what is true.
–Soren Kierkegaard

"Did God actually say . . . ?" (Gen. 3:1)

In the beginning there were no questions of identity (*Who am I?*), no cries for intimacy (*Who will love me?*) and no confusion of purpose (*Why am I here?*). Questions and yearnings of the soul were unknown to Adam and Eve; they knew why they existed and how they were to live. They knew what it meant to be loved and to be the object of someone's delight. Together, the first man and woman knew life as a continuous experience of God's presence and His loving attention. Yes, life in the garden was good. There was food in abundance, labor with a purpose and companionship for life. But the "good life" for Adam and Eve went beyond the visible and physical. God also provided for their inner life. Soul-significance, soul-security and soul-satisfaction came naturally as they walked and talked with God in the garden. Image-bearing flowed naturally in the way they related to each other and to the world around them.

God also gave Adam and Eve freedom. He did not intend for His highest creation to be mindless servants. He gave them the ability to think and reason and, as a result, to discover, reflect, analyze and create. A mind that could think for itself could also choose for itself. God knew this and wanted it for them. As C.S. Lewis so aptly stated in *Mere Christianity*,

> "A world of automata—or creatures that worked like machines—would hardly be worth creating. The happiness which God designs for His higher creatures is the happiness of being freely, voluntarily united to Him and to each other in an ecstasy of love and delight compared with which the most rapturous love between a man and a woman on this earth is mere milk and water. And for that they must be free."[1]

Adam and Eve moved about freely in the newly created world, and they were learning more about it every day. They certainly had the best possible teacher. God was loving, but He was also wise in the ways of life. Both loving and wise, God knew what was best for them and what was best was not everything that was available. This was made clear to Adam from an early conversation about life in the garden. God knew that a certain tree produced fruit with deadly consequences and made sure that Adam understood that fruit from this tree was off limits. He also told Adam why: "Of the tree of the knowledge of good and evil you shall not eat, for in the day that you eat of it you shall surely die" (Gen. 2: 17). Any parent can understand what was behind this prohibition that God made so clear to Adam.

When love says no

We live on the other side of the world from the newest addition to the Sutton clan. Our granddaughter, Hannah, at the time of this writing has just turned one year old. It is not easy to be living so far from our granddaughter, but thanks to modern technology, we are able to see her in action on a regular basis. She is, to be the proud grandparent for a moment, destined to be a mover and shaker. We see this in her, of course, because she is beginning to make her own way in the world now that she has learned to crawl. We see something else as well. Inevitably, the minute a child begins to move and shake anything she can put her hands on, parent-child interactions move into the realm of the negative command.

This has already begun. Scott and Sarah are training Hannah to understand the word "no."

During one memorable online connection, we were watching Hannah crawl across the floor. Actually, we did more than watch. We cheered as we followed her movements from the limited parameters of our computer screen. Clearly, however, Scott and Sarah had a wider and wiser view of the situation. From off the screen came a soft but firm voice.

"No, Hannah."

Hannah kept moving.

"Nooo, Hannah," the voice now slightly less soft and slightly more firm.

At this point, Hannah stopped and looked toward the voice with those big eyes of hers. It was evident to us that she had heard this word in this tone before. Still, she turned away from the voice and kept moving.

"Hannah! NO!"

I am glad to inform you that at this point she stopped her progression. *Yes, dear Hannah*, I mused, *the training has begun. And so has a truth that in life you will not always get what you want. Not even after you have learned to say, "Please."*

But why not? Why the word "no" in increasing accents and louder tones? What was the little cherubic innocent going to do that was so wrong? In this case, potentially electrocute herself by thinking it was okay to play with outlets. Later, her aim might be to pull Mom's laptop off a desk and send it crashing to the floor. Or even later, heaven forbid, release Dad's hand and run into a street of moving traffic. Yes, heaven forbid.

Whenever Scott and Sarah say "No" to Hannah from this point on, it will be to prevent one of two things. It will be to prevent harm to herself in some way, large or small, or prevent harm to something or someone around her (such as denying her the pleasure of hitting some little playmate in the face which, despite cherubic appearance, she may want to do a few years from now). All who enter parenthood learn that "no" is an expression of love, not of wrath nor a petty desire to squelch the fun out of life. In fact, they understand that "no" is an expression of "the fiercest and purest love," as Carolyn Arends writes in her book, *Theology in Aisle Seven: The Uncommon Grace of Everyday Spirituality*.[2] It is protective, not petty. It is a commitment to turn someone you love away from something that will lead to her destruction.

Sometimes it seems a bit petty of God to hold anything back from us. In fact, the world has been making Him out to be an instrument of pettiness and wrath ever since the Great Handover. Yet, "no"—as one learns when on the saying end rather than the hearing—is love in action, not wrath in action. It might look like wrath at the moment, especially to the child whose parent yells an emphatic "NO!" when she is reaching for the handle of a pot on the stove. The child doesn't know it contains boiling water, but the parent does. The "no" sounds harsh to the child but comes from a fierce and protective love in the parent.

Life-giving love was the motivation for the one prohibition that God gave to Adam and Eve in the newly created world. Wisdom—that is, God's understanding of the way things work—and love—His desire for Adam and Eve to live in significance, security and satisfaction—made the prohibition necessary. When Adam and Eve trusted God's love for them and lived by His wisdom, the new world was, in a word, paradise. The occupants had all that was needed for life, and they had a relationship with God that was up close and personal. Questions of identity or purpose and yearnings for love were unknown.

This was Life with a capital L; a "with God" life and a God-designed life. If Adam and Eve lost their creation gifts, it would be their choice, not His.

It did not take them long to choose. The divine paintbrush on the canvas of creation had barely enough time to dry before a choice was made that changed everything. God did not give Adam and Eve away. They gave themselves away and, in so doing, we all lost the life we are meant to live.

The power of a question

"Is that your final answer?" Five simple words are spoken and hundreds or thousands or even a million dollars hang in the balance on the game show *Who Wants to Be a Millionaire?* The contestant is not the only one stressed by this question. Anyone watching the show feels as if he is the one sitting opposite a concerned-looking Regis and is the one about to win or lose. The seconds tick by, a choice is finally made from A, B, C, or D and countless viewers hold their collective breath. But before the answer is revealed, Regis asks The Question once again: *Is that your final answer?* Even someone confident of the answer can be shaken for a second. *He looks so concerned for me. Am I sure? Is this right?*

Perhaps this explains what happened to Eve on that fateful day in the garden. She had not settled on God's Word as her final answer. Despite what she knew of God, a simple question, "Did God really say?" put doubt in her mind. "The deceit, the lie of the devil," writes Dietrich Bonhoeffer, "consists of this, that he wishes to make man believe that he can live without God's word."[3] This was exactly what Satan accomplished when he put himself in Eve's path that day. It is interesting to note that the existence of God was not part of the question. Eve could not be deceived on that point and Satan knew it. Since she literally walked and talked with God, she would have to question her own eyes and ears to question His existence. The target was not belief in God but belief in His word.

Did God really say . . . ? With a simple question, Satan planted doubt in Eve's mind. The question was a well-aimed sword thrust into the newly created soul's place of security. It was designed to destroy everything Eve rested on. Once doubt of God's word was accepted, other doubts would follow. His love for her, His understanding of what she needed in order to be fulfilled, His warnings and His counsel—all could no longer be trusted. To return to the words of Bonhoeffer, if God's word was not true, then one could live without it.

The cunning of Satan's choice to target Eve's trust in God's word is clear when we remember the creation account and the association of God's integrity with His spoken word. To feel the sword thrust, it helps to read the first chapter of Genesis aloud and listen with the soul to the words that occur over and over: "God said . . . and there was . . . God said . . . it was so . . ." This is our God. Powerful and sure in all that He says. This is someone we can lean on and know that as we lean, we will not fall. Then read the beginning of Genesis chapter three to catch the import of Satan's question. Satan's first weapon against the newly created soul was a question aimed at the integrity of God's word.

"Did God actually say . . . ?" The soul's destruction would begin in a place of security: God's word. Satan's weapon was a question designed to plant the lie that God cannot be trusted. The question worked.

The power of a suggestion

After shaking Eve's confidence in God, and in the process destroying her security, Satan's second thrust was aimed at her God-designed place of satisfaction. A second lie was planted in the soul, this time not by a question but by a suggestion. "When you eat of it [the fruit]," Satan told Eve, "your eyes will be opened, and you will be like God" (Gen. 3:5). *Which is to say, Eve, you may think life as you know it is good, but you don't see things as they really are. In fact, you don't see yourself as you really are. God may say you have all you need, but you are lacking something. You are deficient "as is." You need something more than what God has given you. Of course, you obviously do not know, because God hasn't told you, but I am telling you now. Eat this fruit, and you will see what you have been missing.*

"Deficient 'as is.'" "Not enough." "You need something more." "God is holding back on you." "His terms are too restrictive, so reach for life on your own terms." Eve listened to the voice of the enemy of her soul, and life was never the same. What choices did Eve make when she listened to Satan, reached for the forbidden fruit and then handed it to Adam? She chose to:

- Believe the enemy of her soul rather than the lover of her soul.
- Doubt God's Word to her and His love for her.
- Enhance self-image rather than rest in bearing God's image.
- Reach for life terms rather than live by God's.

To extend Eve grace, she most likely had no idea that she was having a conversation with her soul's worst enemy. She could not know what she was unleashing on the world by ignoring God's terms and reaching for the fruit. Generations of wounded and scarred souls and broken and devastated lives have known only too well and too personally what a knowledge of evil in the human soul would make possible in the world, but Eve only knew there was something she did not have. Something God had said was not good for her but another voice was suggested otherwise. In her God-designed soul, innocence from evil, she could not know what a knowledge of evil would mean. Satan knew, of course, and this is what he was after, a world under his terms rather than God's.

Eve also did not know of the *soul death* that would come from eating the fruit. She did not know it would disconnect her soul from its very source of life. Satan knew that Eve could not be like God without God, but he left that bit of information out of the conversation. His aim was to destroy Godlikeness, not create it. Eve thought she was reaching for a better way to live. Instead, she lost the only way she could live. In his book *The Gift of Being Yourself*, David Benner describes it this way: "The core of the lie that Adam and Eve believed was that they could be like God without God."[4]

Satan used Eve to get what he wanted for himself, a kingdom of God-deniers. If the scene in the garden were captured on video, I imagine the camera would first zoom in on Eve's hand reaching for the fruit, then it would move to the serpent watching her hand, focusing on his eyes gleaming with satisfaction. What Satan could not get in heaven, he would get on earth. The human heart and mind would be his to rule on earth, and the soul would be his for eternity. Not being God, of course, he could not know the future nor could he know God's plan for restoration. All he knew was *mission accomplished*. Not a bad day's work.

If Eve had known she was chatting with someone whose intention was to destroy her for eternity, not to mention the whole of the human race to follow, she might have walked away on the spot. Or maybe not. That we will never know. What we do know is that she made a choice to live apart from God's word. She moved from a God-focus to a self-focus. Instead of finding the better life that Satan had suggested would come, she destroyed the designer-life that she had.

Eve was not alone in her choice to ignore God's spoken word. The Genesis account notes that Adam was with her at the time. Adam knew exactly what God had said about this particular tree. In fact, it was during his own one-on-one conversation with God when the command was given.

When Eve misquoted God, Adam could have corrected her. He could have encouraged her to trust God rather than to doubt Him. He could have pulled her away from the serpent and said, "Let's ask God about this. Maybe there's something we don't fully understand yet." But Adam did neither of these things. Rather than clinging to what he knew to be true, Adam remained silent and accepted the offered fruit. He too reached for life on his own terms and moved his loyalty from God to himself.

The handover of the soul severed the soul's connection with God. The results were serious. A disregard of God's command brought swift and sure devastation. As a result of Adam and Eve's choice, sin entered the newly created soul. It affected them immediately and was unleashed into the world to affect every soul to follow.

Sin is a word we don't like to use these days. It is considered old-fashioned and, if we use it, might land us in a religious camp that puts us in unfavorable light with our neighbors. And heaven forbid that we should be seen in an unfavorable light by anyone (except that heaven did not forbid this). However, sin is a reality, no matter how we feel about it. Sin is destructive. It not only harms us but also can harm those around us. It has consequences, including eternal ones.

God knew this, which was why He said "no" to one thing in the garden. That one thing was a particularly destructive thing in the newly created world, but it was still one thing. And, yet, out of all the "yeses" that surrounded Adam and Eve, they moved toward the one "no." They stuck their fingers in the forbidden outlet. They reached for the pot. They darted away from the hand that held them and ran into the busy street.

Carolyn Arends writes: "What if God grieves sin less because it offends his sensibilities and more because he hates the way it distorts our perceptions and separates us from him?"[5] What if, I add, we begin to see that when God says no to something, He is not denying us what is good but protecting us from what will destroy? What if underlying everything He commands is a knowledge of what leads to death and what leads to life, and a love so passionate and committed that He cares enough to tell us which is which?

Something died on this day in the garden. In fact, several things died. The possibility of eternal life died when sin came into the world, making us truly lost souls for eternity, as well as the possibility of life as we are meant to live it in the here and now. The real you and the real me are made to live in connection with God and, we cannot be our true selves without this connection. We cannot be image-bearers without it. What is left then for us? In the next chapter we will see that when we are no longer able to be image-bearers, we become image-projectors instead.

Real Life with a Real God

"Now what was the sort of 'hole' man had got himself into? He had tried to set up on his own, to behave as if he belonged to himself."–C. S. Lewis[6]

1. Read the account of the Great Handover in Genesis 3.
2. What is true and what is false in the serpent's conversation with Eve? What tactics did the enemy of the soul use to persuade Eve to disobey God?
3. How do these same tactics keep you from full surrender and trust in your relationship with God? Reflect on the following questions:

- In what ways do I believe Satan's lies that God cannot be trusted or that I am deficient as God created me? How does believing these lies keep me from resting in His word?
- What "voices" do I listen to more than God's voice speaking through His Word? (consider the voices of media, friends, family, work colleagues, etc.)
- To whom am I looking at this time for my deepest security and satisfaction?

4. The following verses speak of the soul. As you read them, let God speak to you, then tell Him what is on your heart in response to what you read.

Ps. 62:1, 5–8   Matt. 11:28–29
Jer. 6:16   Matt. 16:24–26

5

Keeping Up Appearances

My soul that was at rest now resteth not,
For I am with myself and not with thee.–George MacDonald[1]

They exchanged the truth about God for a lie and worshiped and
served the creature rather than the Creator. (Rom. 1:25)

The ancient Hebrews had an interesting concept of human nature that is rooted, I believe, in the Great Handover. According to Hebrew thought, the human psyche has two natures: the inner self, described as "what we are to ourselves," and the outer self, described as "how we appear to those who observe us." We live simultaneously in both worlds, that of our outer self which others observe, and our inner self which we alone know to be true about us; yet it is possible for the two to be quite different.

How we appear to those who observe us may not match what we know we truly are. Sometimes the difference between outward appearance and inward reality is as simple and harmless as appearing to be happy about the party we're invited to on Friday evening when what we really want to do is stay home and read a book. Sometimes the difference is more complex and more damaging.

This past week, in a span of just three days, I have heard of two arrests. Two men in two countries have been put in prison, one for sexual abuse of children, the other for physical abuse of a wife and daughter. Such news is always sad to hear but is particularly sad when we know the person. I have met one of these men and friends of ours knew the other. They are not men whom one would say upon hearing of an arrest, "I'm not surprised." Both were involved in church ministries. Both have qualities which one values in friendship as well as in ministry. The shock and confusion one feels when someone you know turns out to be different from what you thought can run deep. Naturally, questions arise. Can I trust anyone these days? Who else has something hidden away and nurtured in secret places while presenting a different face to the world?

For the vast majority of us, the consequences of a disconnection between outward appearance and inward reality are not so far reaching, but differences between the two, no matter how large or small, were never meant to be. We are created for wholeness, and this includes a wholeness, or integrity, in how we live. Outward realities match inward realities that, without any pretense, is a true picture of who we are.

The Hebrew word which defines the inner self is *nepesh*. It means at its root "to breathe." God breathed life into Adam[2] and he became *nepesh* or a living, breathing being (see Gen. 2:7). Think of the intimacy implied in this creation act of God breathing life into Adam. Imagine the closeness that such an action required. The first person Adam would see as he opened his eyes was God. His first awareness of an existence outside of himself was God. The life coursing through his body, now living, was due to God and God alone, and he knew it. From the beginning Adam knew that his soul, his mind, his heart and everything given life in his body belonged to his creator.

Nepesh is translated in various places by various words such as soul, spirit, mind, person, or self but to the Hebrew mind, it simply meant who we are in our inmost being. We are more than a physical life with a beating heart, expanding lungs, flowing blood, active cells and genetic tendencies. We have a *soul life*, with an ability to think and reason, desire and dream, be purposeful and intentional. For the soul to live, it must be God-breathed and God-connected.

In contrast to *nepesh*, the word defining the outward self is *shem* and has to do with external appearances. *Shem* literally means "name" or "fame,"[3] two words which suggest one's reputation in the eyes of the world. Whether we like it or not, we gain a reputation by how we appear to others.

My mind goes back to my freshman year in college, and life on the third floor of Joyner residence hall, where I lived during my first year at the University of North Carolina in Chapel Hill. It soon became apparent that many of the students on my floor, newly released from the yoke of home, were bent on making a name for themselves in their new environment, a name which often had nothing to do with the Dean's List that appeared at the end of each semester. Other reputations than academic honor were sought in the new found freedom of university life. The biggest drinker, the latest sleeper, the one with the most dates on the weekend, the wildest partier—these pursuits often produced interesting conversations on stairwells at three o'clock in the morning.

I enjoyed college life immensely and sleeping late was as true of me as the others on my floor, although not to gain a reputation. I needed the extra sleep to balance out my late night studies in the library. Sleepless nights and consequently, late mornings, may account for a reputation I gained without even trying. Some years after graduating, a student who had known me in Chapel Hill met my father at a social gathering. Understandably, they connected on the one point they had in common: me. Their conversation, strangely enough, turned to the topic of procrastination. (My father seemed to relish telling me this when we were together afterward.) It seems that my friend had remarked that he often saw me dashing out of the dormitory at what seemed breathless speeds. I suggested to Dad that an ability to focus on what was in front of me was the reason for those last-minute rushes to class, but I am sure he knew better, having observed me closely up to that point for twenty-five years. A reputation for procrastination was born from how I appeared to those who observed me.

We want to be seen in a favorable light so naturally we give thought to how we appear to others. This is not just for our own sakes but out of respect for others and deference to the various situations we are in. Dressing appropriately for formal occasions is a good idea even if we prefer jeans and a hoodie. It is certainly advisable to arrive on time for class or for a meeting even if we do not live our lives by the clock. Paying attention to outward appearance and outward behavior is wise but only if we pay equal attention to what is happening in the soul. Many a reputation has ridden to heights of fame and glory on the basis of outward behavior and appearance, only to crash when outward appearance is not in line with inward realities.

Both *nepesh* and *shem* are part of our God-designed nature, and there is meant to be integrity between the two, just as there is integrity between all of God's names and His character. We can take any of God's names—Jehovah-Roi (Shepherd),[4] Jehovah-Jireh (Provider),[5] Jehovah-Rapha (Healer),[6] Jehovah-Shalom (Peace),[7] to name a few—and know that He is true to His name and reputation. We, too, are meant for integrity of our inner character matching our outward reputation, but something happened on the day of the Great Handover which caused a separation between the two.

Before the handover and disconnection of the soul, there was no need for a distinction between an inner and outer life, quite simply, because there was no distinction. Adam and Eve's outward-focused life—the life that interacted with the world around them, related to each other, cared for the earth and its inhabitants, and made a myriad of decisions on a daily basis—flowed from their inner God-connected soul. They were whole as human beings. They were a man and woman of integrity because there was no separation between outward appearance and inward reality.

For Adam and Eve, life in the world flowed from life with God, and this included how they related to each other. There was no need to be self-conscious because they did not need each other to validate their worth or to fill empty spaces in the soul. God had already validated them, and He filled their souls. Personal significance and worth, personal security and sense of identity—all of these were ingrained and natural to them. They could relate to each other without using each other for their own needs.

So when Scripture tells us that "the eyes of both were opened, and they knew that they were naked" (Gen. 3:7), we understand that something deeper than physical awareness was at work. Their physical bodies had not changed. They were naked before and, not being physically blind, had observed this with their physical eyes. What changed after eating the fruit was more fundamental than physical observation. Sin had entered the world and severed their souls from its God-connected life. Losing God, they lost their place of significance, security and satisfaction. Having been created by God for these, they still felt the need for them and equally felt their lack. Instead of going immediately to God, however, to confess what had happened and seek restoration, they left God out of the picture altogether. How easily and quickly we leave God out of the picture. How easily and quickly we turn elsewhere for solutions to our souls' needs. Instead of looking to God, Adam and Eve looked to each other for significance, security and satisfaction. When they did, self-consciousness made its debut into the world.

The first self-conscious move was to distance themselves from each other. They did this physically by sewing fig leaves to cover their bodies. With a little feminine intuition, it is easy to imagine that Eve did not like what she saw, at least as much as she could see of herself, and she naturally thought Adam would not like it either. Satan's lie, which had enticed her to reach for the fruit, was now firmly planted in her mind. Deficient "as is" was the new awareness, not loved "as is." Adam must have felt the same since they both spent time hiding their nakedness. Self-consciousness replaced God-consciousness in defining how they felt about themselves and how they lived in the world. Self-consciousness made them no longer sure of themselves and no longer sure of each other and so the cover-up began.

The next self-conscious move was to distance themselves from God. This was done by hiding from God both physically and spiritually. Here the Genesis record makes fascinating reading from a psychological point of view. Keeping up appearances moves quickly from a relational to a spiritual matter when God asks Adam, "Have you eaten of the tree of which I commanded you not to eat?" (3:11). Adam could not deny that he had eaten the fruit, but he could shift God's attention away from himself to Eve and make himself appear less to blame. Eve was a quick learner and in turn blamed the serpent. Something was wrong, that was obvious, but it was not their fault. Someone else was to blame. Adam and Eve attempted to hide spiritually from God by hiding their inner brokenness behind an outward appearance of blamelessness. They moved quickly from being image-*bearers* to image-*projectors*, feeling the need to *project an appearance of morality* even if it was not the reality. The Great Handover became the Great Disconnect of the soul from God, which led to the Great Cover-Up.

Image-projecting versus image-bearing

Modern writers and teachers on spiritual formation give a name to this way of relating to the world, which began when the soul lost its God-connection. They call it the "false self." The term rings true when we remember that there is a true self, a God-connected, God-believing, image-bearing self, which we are no longer able to be after the handover. While the true self derives its identity from God, the false self "must cobble together an identity from secondary things: reputation, success, status, family, jobs, health," as Adele Ahlberg Calhoun notes in her *Spiritual Disciplines Handbook.*[8] David Benner puts it this way: "With the self that is created in God's likeness rejected, our false self is the self we develop in our own likeness," a self that depends on what we have, what we can do, and what others think of us.[9]

G. K. Chesterton, that witty and wise lay theologian and writer of the last century, related this new human condition of the false self to a type of spiritual amnesia:

> "We have all read in scientific books and, indeed, in all romances, the story of the man who has forgotten his name. This man walks about the streets and can see and appreciate everything; only he cannot remember who he is. Well, every man is that man in the story. Every man has forgotten who he is. . . .We are all under the same mental calamity; we have all forgotten our names. We have all forgotten what we really are."[10]

Chesterton, in his own words, says the same things as modern Christian writers. We have lost our true selves, and we have lost this so much that we have forgotten completely how we are supposed to be and how we are supposed to live. Because we have forgotten who we are, we cannot live as we are meant to live.

No longer able to be our true selves as God-designed image-bearers, we become a "false self," and live as image-projectors. That is, we seek to project images of significance, satisfaction and security, which come from something outside of ourselves and are based on something other than God.

Without a God-connected soul to define who we are, help us to know who and what to believe, give us perspective

on life and shape how we live in the world, we turn to
external connections, images and voices to define and shape
us. The world gladly and intentionally flings images at us
on a daily basis, largely through the media but also through
the people around us. We follow after them, hoping that we
will be as successful, as significant, as beautiful, as valued, as
worthy of notice and worthy of love as the images and voices
suggest we can be if we will only be like them.

Self-focus entered the world on the heels of sin and oust-
ed the security and restfulness of soul which comes from a
God-focused life. Along with self-focus came an entire clan
of clinging cousins to take up residence in the now God-va-
cant soul: self-pity, self-defense, self-promotion, self-doubt,
self-indulgence, self-importance, self-will, self-righteousness,
self-satisfaction, self-service, self-protection and self-deception. A soul separated from God and filled with self-centeredness can live no other way than by image-projection.

What is the difference between image-projectors and
image-bearers? How does this "look" as we live in the world?

- *Image-projectors* are concerned about what others
  know and see; *image-bearers* are concerned about
  what God knows and sees.

- *Image-projectors* focus on maintaining an image in
  the world; *image-bearers* focus on maintaining a relationship with God.

- *Image-projectors* relate to others in ways that main-
  tain control; *image-bearers* relate to others from their
  place of restful trust in God.

- An *image-projector's* core belief is "I am what others
  think or say about me"; an *image-bearer's* core belief
  is "I am what God thinks and says about me."

- *Image-projectors* cannot rest; they must be successful or productive or thin or beautiful or healthy or witty to feel significant, and this takes a lot of work.
- *Image-bearers* are active; there are jobs to do and relationships to nurture; they care about their health and about how they look; but are restful in the soul, because they find value and significance in being known, loved and sustained by God.

Does anything in this list resonate with you? It does with me. My heart responds with a strong "yes" to knowing and living from where my true value lies, to leaving behind a life of image-projection and becoming the image-bearer I am meant to be. But I cannot do this on my own. You cannot—not with souls remain disconnected from their source of life and minds that suffer from spiritual amnesia, not when we are lost and far from home. Only God can reclaim what was lost; only He can restore His image in us.

And so we come full circle. The Great Handover that ushered in the Great Disconnect and led to the Great Cover-Up becomes the Great Restoration. God's passionate and pursuing love makes possible what we cannot do for ourselves by sending His Son to reclaim souls that belong to Him and restore the things that were broken.

Reversing the choice

Jesus, God the eternal Word, was present at the Great Handover. He saw first hand what choices were made and what was lost for eternity. We should not be surprised that in His teaching He asks a question which echoes what He witnessed that day: "For what does it profit a man if he gains the whole world and loses or forfeits himself?" (Luke 9:25). Nor should we be surprised when Jesus declares that restoration happens only when we reverse the choices that led to the fatal handover: "Whoever loves his life loses it, and whoever hates his life in this world will keep it for eternal life" (John 12:25).

When we understand the choices that severed our divine connection and brought sin with its devastating consequences into the world, Jesus' words make sense. He speaks from what He knows is true.

The creator alone has the right to declare the purpose of a new creation. Leslie thoughtfully and carefully brings clay to life, bearing an image in her mind until it becomes something real in her hands. She knows best what her creations need in order to fulfill their purpose. Some pieces of pottery cannot be put in a dishwasher or they will crack and break. I have no problem with what Leslie says is necessary for her creations to function at their best.

Our best life and our true life is possible only when we live in the dignity and purpose God has bestowed on us. William Temple wrote in his treatise on *Christianity and Social Order*, published in 1942, "Our dignity is that we are children of God, capable of communion with God, the object of the love of God—displayed to us on the cross—and destined for eternal fellowship with God. Our true value is not what we are worth in ourselves but what we are worth to God, and that worth is bestowed upon us by the utterly gratuitous love of God."[11]

God's vision for us in Christ is not only redemption from sin that separates us from life with Him but also restoration of the life we are created to live. He envisions our return to the real you and the real me. We are created to belong, but sin separated us from the One who created and loves us. We are created to be image-bearers, but sin marred the image of God within. Jesus' death on the cross dealt with sin once and for all and opened the way again for life with God. Significance and security are possible once again. His resurrection after the cross gives us a living Lord who restores us to the family likeness. No separation between inner reality and outer appearance. No image-projecting and maintaining appearances; only image-bearing and being real.

Real Life with a Real God:

"When we seek to root our being in something other than God, we are false self."–Robert Mulholland[12]

1. Reflect on the following verses which relate to keeping up appearances:

   1 Sam. 16:7   Matt. 23:25–28
   Isa. 29:13–16 (cf: Matt 15:1–9)   Gal. 2:6

2. Our souls are constantly being conditioned by the society in which we live and by the messages we receive from it.
   a. What is conditioning my soul?
   b. Do I live under a sign that says "Not enough"? (not thin enough, smart enough, patient enough, loving enough, successful enough, etc.).
   c. Fill in the phrase "I am not _____enough" to name the areas where "deficient as is" is at work in your life.
   d. Take time to release the images of beauty, body shape, health, house neatness, business, ministry success, leadership, etc., that you carry in your mind.

3. How does Jesus enable us to move from image-projection to being image-bearers once again according to the following verses?

   John 7:38–39   Hebrews 1:3
   2 Corinthians 3:18   Colossians1:15–17, 27

4. In Galatians 1:10, Paul asks a question of himself and the Christian community. Read this verse and reflect on the question. It may be helpful to review the list of self and its clinging cousins found in this chapter. Which of these are active in your life? Spend time talking with God about the image-projecting you see in your own life or even in your church community at this time.

5. Reflect on the following words by Robert McGee: "If we know who we are, we will not try to become someone else in order to have value and meaning in our lives. If we don't know who we are, we will try to become someone who someone else wants us to be!"[13] How does this speak to you?

6

Pursuing Love

Here you have the one great desire of God that moved him in the work of redemption: His heart longed for man, to dwell with him and in him.–Andrew Murray[1]

For the Son of Man came to seek and to save the lost. (Luke 19:10)

God's passionate and pursuing love makes possible what we cannot do for ourselves. He sent His Son on a rescue mission to reclaim souls that belong to Him and to restore the things that were broken. It takes passion and commitment to reclaim and restore what is lost to us, especially against great odds. Louis and I have seen such passion and commitment in the country of Chad where we served as missionaries for thirteen years.

Chad is surrounded by some rather unfriendly neighbors. Not long before our family arrived in Chad, one of these neighbors, Libya, invaded from the north and captured a stretch of land across the edge of the Sahara called the Aouzou Strip. Why Libya wanted a piece of desert defies reason, but they took this region of Chad by force and established a military presence. Chad has neither the wealth nor the military strength to equal Libya, but even so, not long after the invasion, Chadian soldiers won back their land. We became friends with a soldier who was present on that day of victory and learned from him how it happened.

The Libyan army had buried mines throughout the edge of the occupied land and then placed Soviet tanks along its border with their turrets facing south. The Chadian army had nothing on its side but pickup trucks. They were facing great odds, to say the least. But they had one thing that gave them an advantage over the enemy—a passion for what was theirs. The only question was how to gain it back.

When you have very little to work with, you use what you have. Someone came up with the idea of attaching anti-tank guns to the back of pickup trucks and counting on reckless courage to get the trucks and the soldiers in them past the mines. The strategy? Drivers would simply "put the pedal to the metal" and drive the trucks at such incredible speeds across the sand that even when hidden mines were triggered, the trucks were able to speed past them by the time they exploded. Pickup trucks and passion won the day.

Every driver knew that as long as his truck moved at extreme speeds, he would be successful, but if he hesitated even for a moment, the result would be deadly. As my husband is fond of observing when he relates this story, if ever the proverb "he who hesitates is lost" had any meaning, it was on this day.

The strategy was reckless and seemingly foolish, but it worked. Our friend was one of the military drivers that day. With a gleam in his eyes, he described the exhilaration of flying across the sand at breakneck speed and hearing mines explode right and left behind him. After crossing the mined zone, the pickup trucks zipped in and out like hornets among the heavy Soviet tanks whose turrets moved too slowly to do much damage in return. On that day, with nothing but anti-tank guns attached to the back of pickup trucks and courage fueled by passion, the Chadians forced the Libyans out of the desert and off their land.

The Chadians did not have Black Hawk helicopters or scud missiles to fight against mines and tanks. They did not have what the Western world would consider adequate military training, but they had two things which gave them an advantage over the enemy—a passion for what was theirs and a determination to reclaim what was lost.

Louis and I were impressed and, quite honestly, amazed at what our friend was willing to do in order to reclaim what belonged to his country. We had to admit that it seemed foolish in our eyes for him to take such a risk, even when we knew the end of the story. It also reminded us of another rescue mission that seemed foolish to the world but ended in victory. "For the word of the cross is folly to those who are perishing, but to us who are being saved it is the power of God" (1 Cor. 1:18). This rescue mission was playing for much greater stakes than a piece of land in the desert. Our Chadian friend's passion, although justifiable and admirable, was for something temporal. The physical world will not last forever. The Aouzou strip of the Sahara Desert will one day cease to exist. Scripture tells us that there exists an object of passion which does last forever, and there is a deeper passion that moved heaven and earth to reclaim it.

The Chadians' passion for what was rightfully theirs sped them across land mines. Even so, as our friend acknowledged, every soldier hoped in his heart to return from the battle alive. God sent His Son through space and time to reclaim the object of His passion, knowing that the battle for our souls would be won only when His Son died on a cross.

The cause of His journey

Teresa of Avila wrote in the sixteenth century, "May God grant us the ability to see how much we cost him."[2] A line in Mozart's Requiem, written two centuries later, breathes a haunting prayer that is reminiscent of her words: "Remember, merciful Jesu, that I am the cause of your journey." Because of the sin unleashed in the world by Eve's and Adam's choices and because of the disconnection of the soul that sin has produced, we are the cause of an incredible journey.

Romantic tales of a prince slashing through forests of thickly twisted branches to awaken a sleeping princess do not come close to the very real journey that Jesus made at the Father's request to restore life to us. For one thing, we are not asleep and blissfully unaware of our comatose state like the princess in the fairy tale. We are, to be blunt, more like science fiction stories of the walking dead, moving around with a semblance of life but giving the distinct impression that all is not as it should be.

Jesus made an incredible journey to set things right in the world. The world, however, had no idea who had just arrived on its doorstep in a small town in Palestine. By this time in history, God was relegated by some cultures to "the man upstairs" or—in the case of the Greeks and Romans—to a group of men and women upstairs who capriciously ruled the affairs of men. Other cultures were controlled by fear of a multitude of gods who were more demonic than benevolent while still others completely denied the existence of a personal God. Even in Israel, men and women who believed in the true God kept a respectful distance while only their religious leaders approached Him in the temple.

Adam and Eve walked with God in the garden and spoke with Him face to face, but by the time God entered the world in the form of the Son, spiritual amnesia had indeed settled in. It was a sad reflection on the state of the world that "[Jesus] was in the world, and the world was made through him, yet the world did not know him. He came to his own, and his own people did not receive him" (John 1:10–11). This is how far we had moved from intimacy. This is how much we had forgotten whose we were. Deeply committed to the soul's relationship with God, Jesus gave up everything He knew and gave all of Himself to bring us home.

Leaving it all behind

Movies on the death and resurrection of Christ have given us visual images of what it cost Jesus to physically die for us. But His suffering for our sake went beyond the physical. Jesus suffered the loss of everything He had known when He stepped out of eternity into time.

I cannot wrap my mind around eternity. It is impossible even with my vivid imagination to grasp what coming to earth meant to God. I will not know until I reach heaven and see for myself what glories Jesus left behind or what intimacy between the Father, Son and Holy Spirit was laid aside for a moment in time. The following illustration, however, helps me try.

Imagine growing up on a farm with spacious fields to roam and miles of woods to explore. The farm extends as far as your eyes can see and beyond the border is nothing but open sky. You live outdoors most of the day and relish an existence where nothing limits you. Space, light and freedom fill your soul with incredible joy every day.

Then imagine leaving that farm at your father's request to live in a cement room in a nearby city. The room itself is quite large. It has a high ceiling. There is even space enough to stand and move about. Lining one side of the room is a standing replica of a forest, and it is quite realistic. Fields beyond are painted in three-dimensional art on the walls and a blue sky with clouds is painted on the ceiling. But the sky lacks depth and pure air. The trees lack their true color. You can even walk among them, but you miss the feel and the smell of the real thing. Despite the size of the room, it feels enclosed and not quite . . . right. Imagine this, and you might have an idea of what it meant for Jesus to leave heaven and live for a time on earth.

My imagination is admittedly influenced by C.S. Lewis' conclusion to the *Chronicles of Narnia* in *The Last Battle* where his main characters walk through a door and discover a world which seems more real and more vibrant than the one they have just left. As they walk in further, it finally dawns on them that they are still in Narnia, and that what they have known up to that point was merely a shadow. Now they are experiencing the real thing.

Narnia is a fictional place in a good story, but Lewis' imagery of the brighter, truer Narnia symbolizes a very real heaven. At the Father's request, Jesus left the spacious, vibrant glory of heaven to live a confined existence on earth. Not only did He leave such glory for such limitations, but He embarked on the journey knowing that it would end with an agonizing death. Only an incredible love could make such an incredible journey.

We meet the real God in Jesus, and we see this incredible love in action. We have the privilege of listening in on conversations between Jesus and others while He lived among us, thanks to the written records of four men known as Matthew, Mark, Luke and John. In one of these conversations, recorded in the third chapter of John, Jesus reveals the heart that set Him on a journey, and in that heart, we find love.

God so loved

A man came to Jesus in the night with questions on his mind and a hunger in his soul. Like many people in churches today, Nicodemus already knew about Jesus. He knew what Jesus taught and knew what Jesus could do. Nicodemus had stood in the crowds who listened to Jesus and observed Him, but up to this point, his listening and observations were always from a polite and respectful distance. Now it seemed that knowing Jesus from a distance was not enough for Nicodemus. He wanted to see and talk with the man himself. Nicodemus took the first step towards Life with a capital L by meeting up close and personal with the real God.

The beginning of the conversation was respectful and complimentary. "Rabbi," Nicodemus began, "we know that you are a teacher come from God, for no one can do these signs that you do unless God is with him" (John 3:2). Jesus heard the politely distant words but recognized a seeking heart beneath them and moved the conversation swiftly from how He performed on the street to what He wanted to do in Nicodemus's heart.

One verse from the ensuing conversation has become perhaps the most familiar Bible verse in the world because it states simply and clearly the message of the gospel: "For God so loved the world, that he gave his only Son, that whoever believes in him should not perish but have eternal life." Most Christians can quote John 3:16 from memory as easily as we quote familiar advertising slogans, such as "You deserve a break today" or "Just do it." Yet the words that Jesus spoke to Nicodemus are more than an advertising slogan to be glibly rolled off the tongue at a moment's notice, put on posters, woven into songs and printed on t-shirts. The world's destiny hinges on the truth revealed in John 3:16. They contain, as J. I. Packer states "the most wonderful message the world has ever heard, or will hear."[3]

In a conversation with Nicodemus, Jesus reveals the motivation for His journey. It is a journey that began in the heart of God. Love for the world, not condemnation of it, brought Jesus here and sent Him to the cross. What kind of love would go that far? Not a shallow love, that's for sure, and not any kind of love that we can find here on earth. Only a divine love would make such a journey and such a sacrifice.

A God-kind of love

The Old Testament words for love—*ahab*, passionate and pursuing, and *hesed*, merciful and compassionate—are personified in Jesus. He came to the world because of God's passionate and merciful love for us, nothing more and nothing less. The New Testament word that describes the love which sent Jesus on a mission of redemption and restoration is *agapao*. Translated into English equivalents, *agapao* means "to love, esteem, cherish, favor, honor, respect, accept, prize, relish; to be devoted to."[4] These are wonderful words. Life-giving words. Who doesn't want to be esteemed, cherished, favored, honored, respected, accepted and prized by someone else? Who doesn't think at some point, "I wish there was someone devoted to me for a change"?

Someone is devoted to us. Only a love that prized us this greatly and cherished us this deeply could make such a journey. Only devotion as complete as God's devotion to His creation could keep loving even when rejected time and time again. We cannot fully understand the depth of God's love for us or appreciate the immensity of what happened on the cross until we realize how little we deserved it.

Throughout history, God's love pursues a people who reject Him time and again. God-love says to the people of Israel: *We used to have a good thing going, but you rejected Me. In fact, you seem to hate Me by the way you're acting. You ignore everything I say. You look in My direction only when you want something from Me. You pursue other lovers like a prostitute let loose on an oil rig, and there's a bad smell around you of something dead. The smell comes from so deep inside of you that you can't erase it even if you wanted to. This is who you are, and I love you. I want you with Me. I know who you are meant to be, and I know what is possible for you when you are wholly Mine. I know how to erase the smell and make you beautiful again. I love you so much that I am willing to die to make this possible.*

Such unconditional and transforming love is not possible in the human experience. It is a divine love and found only in God. After the soul's disconnection from its divine lover, this kind of love is not possible for us apart from divine intervention. Which is just what God did by bringing His unconditional, transforming and divine love to us in the form of Jesus nailed to a cross. J. I. Packer expresses the immensity of God-love in this way:

It is staggering that God should love sinners; yet it is true. God loves creatures who have become unlovely and (one would have thought) unlovable. There was nothing whatever in the objects of His love to call it forth; nothing in man could attract or prompt it. Love among men is awakened by something in the beloved, but the love of God is free, spontaneous, unevoked, uncaused. God loves men because He has chosen to love them. . . . The Greek and Roman world of New Testament times had never dreamed of such love; its gods were often credited with lusting after women, but never with loving sinners; and the New Testament writers had to introduce what was virtually a new Greek word *agape* to express the love of God as they knew it.[5]

Old Testament history unfolds the story of a love so deep that the Divine Lover untiringly moves toward His people even while they repeatedly move away from Him. The New Testament records the culmination of a love so strong that the Lover dies on a cross for the one He loves. The following words are from Paul's letter to a first-century church. Read them with the expanded definitions of *agapao*, savoring each word as a description of God's love for you:

> I have been crucified with Christ. It is no longer I who live, but Christ who lives in me. And the life I now live in the flesh I live by faith in the Son of God, who loved me, (*esteemed me, cherished me, favored me, honored me, respected me, accepted me, prized me*) and gave himself for me. I do not nullify the grace of God, for if righteousness were through the law, then Christ died for no purpose. (Gal. 2:20-21)

If we truly grasp who we are, lost souls suffering from spiritual amnesia and helpless sinners in need of redemption, and equally grasp what God has done for us, redeemed and restored us to our true selves by bringing us back to Himself, we will not take such love lightly. We will not set aside grace, as Paul writes. We will not live as if Jesus died for nothing more than to launch yet another religion into the world. Instead, we will run to Him and throw ourselves into His welcoming embrace. Something like singing will well up from deep within. It will be the sound of a soul returning home.

The heart of the Son

Jesus took Nicodemus from an external discussion of miracles to an internal discussion of the heart. He revealed that a divine love had commanded the mission, and that the Son had come to fulfill it. But was Jesus mindlessly following orders? Another conversation lets us hear Jesus speaking, not of the Father's heart, but of His own. We learn what keeps the Son on such a journey knowing it will end at a cross.

This second conversation is also recorded in John's Gospel. Jesus and His disciples are together in a room set aside for their celebration of the Passover. The meal is finished, and the disciples are recovering from the shock of Jesus taking on the posture of a servant and washing their feet. They are also feeling sobered by His words. Jesus is talking about leaving them and they can't understand what He means. What He's saying about future events makes no sense to their time-bound minds. They have no idea what is ahead for them, but Jesus knows very well what is coming. As He and His closest earthly friends prepare to leave, He knows that He will be arrested, publicly humiliated, tortured cruelly, tried unjustly and then sentenced to die.

It is interesting that God chose to use the brokenness of the world—manipulation and deceit in the religious system of Israel as well as a broken political system—to do His work of healing its brokenness. Jesus knows this; He will suffer from the brokenness He has come to heal. Ahead of Him is emotional, physical and spiritual suffering and a good portion of these will happen even before He is crucified. He is also well aware that Satan, the enemy of the soul, is waiting with bated breath for the fulfillment of his own mission—to keep his hold on the soul and not let the kingdom of God return to the world. Do we not grasp the depth of God's love? Knowing all of this, Jesus still moves toward the cross.

It is a poignant moment between Jesus and His closest earthly companions as He prepares to head for the cross. In this moment of transition between the feast and the arrest, Jesus reveals He is more than a master with disciples or a rabbi with students. He is a Son doing the will of a Father. Knowing all that lies ahead, Jesus says the following words to His disciples as they are about to leave: "I will no longer talk much with you, for the ruler of this world is coming. He has no claim on me, but I do as the Father has commanded me, so that the world may know that I love the Father. Rise, let us go from here" (John 14:30-31).

What does Jesus want the world to learn? That He loves the Father and that love for the Father is behind everything He does, even behind His obedience on the cross. The Great Handover is reversed by the Great Obedience of Jesus moving towards the cross. The heart of Jesus beats in absolute loyalty, absolute obedience and absolute surrender to the will of the Father, making our restoration possible. Yes, the Chadian army showed great courage to win back their land, but every soldier went into battle hoping he would return alive. When Jesus left eternity and boxed Himself in time, He knew that He was leaving the adoration of angels to live a homeless, wandering life. He knew that He would show compassion, declare truth and bring healing to a world that would reject Him. Paul E. Miller rightly says that "When we watch Jesus, we are watching God love us."[6]

Real Life with a Real God

"We see now what it meant for the Son of God to empty Himself and become poor. It meant a laying aside of glory (the real kenosis); a voluntary restraint of power; an acceptance of hardship, isolation, ill-treatment, malice, and misunderstanding; finally, a death that involved such agony—spiritual, even more than physical—that his mind nearly broke under the prospect of it. (See Luke 12:50, and the Gethsemane story.) It meant love to the uttermost for unlovely men, who 'through his poverty, might become rich. . . . It is the most wonderful message that the world has ever heard, or will hear."–J. I. Packer[7]

1. Read the following verses and reflect on God's love for a fallen and lost creation:
   Gen. 3:21   Zeph. 3:14–17
   Deut. 5:32–33; 30:11–20   John 15:13
   Jer. 31:3   Hos. 2:19–23
   Rom. 5:6–8   Eph. 1:4–6; 2:1–5

2. Personalize 1 Pet. 1:8–9 by replacing pronouns, reading *I* in place of *you* and *You* in place of *him* when it refers to Christ. For example, "Though I have not seen You, I love You. Though I do not now see You, I believe in

You." You may find it helpful to write this and then read it aloud.

3. Do the same for Romans 8:31–39 and then tell God what is on your heart in response to His love.

7

Grace and Truth

*The mission undertaken by the Son was not to show Himself as
having all power in heaven and earth, but to reveal His Father,
to show Him to men such as He is, that men may know Him,
and knowing, trust Him.* –George MacDonald[1]

*We have seen his glory, glory as of the only Son from the Father,
full of grace and truth.* (John 1:14)

The subtitle of this book asks a question: what happens when the real you meets the real God? As we read
through the Gospel accounts of Jesus' life on earth, we meet
the real God. We also see real people meeting Him, and in
their interactions we find the answer to the question. Whenever people encounter Jesus, they are changed.

I love to read through all four Gospel accounts, but
John's Gospel is one of my favorites. He seemed to understand Jesus, and this is reflected in the way he writes about
Him. His account of the earthly life and ministry of Jesus
begins with a penetrating insight to the divine identity:

In the beginning was the Word, and the Word was with
God, and the Word was God. He was in the beginning
with God. All things were made through him, and without him was not any thing made that was made. In him

was life, and the life was the light of men. The light shines in the darkness, and the darkness has not overcome it. (John 1:1–5)

John continues his description of Jesus by using two words which describe the real God: "The Word became flesh and dwelt among us, and we have seen his glory, glory as of the only Son from the Father, full of grace and truth" (1:14). Grace and truth. As we read through all the Gospel accounts, we see that Jesus' actions and words are indeed full of grace and truth. He can be nothing else as He relates to the world and to us, for God is always true to His nature. In fact, He has no need to be anything else. There is no one that God needs to impress and no one whose opinion He fears, so He can speak truth and can give grace. God is secure in His image and will always be true to Himself no matter how the world in its brokenness responds to Him. This is important for us to remember for two reasons.

We have a tendency to fashion God out of our own image, which we have seen is now a broken one. The world's brokenness is deep, and this brokenness has distorted God's image in us. It has also distorted our image of God. We are no longer whole, and for the most part, we no longer want a whole God. We prefer a partial God. We would like a God with grace to accept our brokenness but not with truth to transform us.

We also have a tendency to fashion God out of the image of the times in which we live. At various points in history, truth is the focus while at other times grace comes to the forefront. We see this largely through the changing vocabulary of the church. For example, spiritual books and hymns written in the early 20th century often used military vocabulary for the Christian life. This is not surprising when we remember that in the first half of the 20th century the world was shaped by two major wars. There were clear sides of right and wrong in these wars. There was a clear evil at work. Being a soldier for Christ meant recognizing we fight not only earthly battles but spiritual ones. This was readily understood in an age of good versus evil.

Times have changed, and the vocabulary of the church has changed with it. Today, it is not wise to use military terms in reference to the Christian life. Such terms today evoke images of fanaticism and equate religion with acts of aggression. There is wisdom in moving away from a vocabulary which no longer communicates what we mean, but there is also danger in losing something in the shift. We may also move away from essential truths about the world and about God. No matter what vocabulary we use and no matter what age we live in, there is still evil in the world, and God has given us truth to live by.

Today's vocabulary of the church is shaped by psychology rather than war. This focus has affected the church in a positive way. We have begun to admit that we are broken people and that we are in the process of being made whole. Psychology has helped us with a growing understanding of the ways we think and behave and how our past experiences affect the ways we relate in the present. It is a good thing for the church to recognize that we can declare biblical truth but also acknowledge that brokenness affects every person in the world, including a redeemed person in Christ. The Reformation brought a much-needed return to grace in reference to salvation and how we relate to God, but the centuries that followed show little evidence of grace in reference to sanctification and how we relate to each other in the process. Today, we recognize that grace is something we receive from God but also something we give each other as well.

We are broken people in the process of being made whole. We need much grace, and we must extend grace to each other. The danger comes when grace is turned into tolerance, and we suggest that there is no longer a right and wrong way to live.

Presenting a gracious God to the world is easy and makes us no enemies, but it is an incomplete picture and does not lead us toward wholeness. Grace without truth, as God knows, may make us feel good but keeps us broken and in bondage. On the other hand, truth without grace also gives the world an incomplete picture of God. Proclaiming a legalist God who cares for nothing but His standards is a modern form of Pharisaism, insisting that everyone adheres to God's standards without declaring His grace is with us in the process. Grace without truth can leave us in bondage, but truth without grace can wound even more deeply.

The real God is both grace and truth. We see this over and over in the Gospels as we watch real people encounter Jesus and see how their lives are changed.

The real God in action

One of the most poignant and powerful moments of a grace and truth encounter is found in the eighth chapter of John's Gospel where a real woman meets the real God. But she is not the only one changed by this God-encounter. Both the woman caught in sin and the men who accuse her are changed by meeting God up close and personal when they interact with Jesus.

The story is familiar, but I will summarize it briefly. It's early in the morning, and Jesus is once again at the temple surrounded by a crowd of people. He is just about to speak when a group of religious leaders, we are not told how many, push through the crowd and make their way toward Him. They have a woman with them whom they place in front of Jesus in full view of the crowds. They inform Jesus that she has been caught in adultery and remind Him what the law of Moses says to do with such a woman. According to the law, she is to be stoned. What does Jesus say should happen to her?

When I read this part of the story, I think of words of Alexander Pope: "Let not this weak unknowing hand/ Presume Thy bolts to throw."[2] The accusers are certainly presuming to throw God's bolts, but as we read the account, we are aware that they have something more in mind than God's law. They are hoping to trap Jesus. They want Him to say something which would provide them a reason to do away with Him. Jesus is fully aware of their intent. He knows their question is not about God's law nor really about the woman, but about Him. They are using both the woman and the law for their own agenda, which is to bring trouble to Jesus.

If you were one of the disciples with Jesus at this moment, what would you be doing as you watch this encounter? You might be shifting your feet uncomfortably and hoping that Jesus does not break forth into another diatribe against the religious authorities. He is already in trouble for things He has been saying along those lines. Besides, the woman was caught in a sin that is clearly against God's law. Surely this is a no-brainer. Jesus, being God, has more of a right to punish her than the men who brought her to the temple.

She has sinned against Him personally, although neither she nor the men with her understand this as they wait for Jesus to respond.

What is Jesus going to do? Go for grace and teach the legalists a lesson? But this would mean ignoring the standards God has set for His people and condoning adultery. Well then, will He go for truth and teach the woman a lesson? The odds are in favor of this response. She may be broken, but she has probably broken up a family and devastated more lives than her own by her actions. But this would ignore compassion and mercy which are equally in God's nature.

What Jesus does is one of the most beautiful moments in the Gospels, and the Gospels are full of beautiful moments. Jesus says nothing. He does not address the woman or the accusers, at least not initially. He stoops to the ground and begins writing with His finger. One sees an immediate act of grace in this movement as Jesus draws the eyes of the crowd and the accusers away from the woman to Himself. Indeed, all acts of grace begin when eyes are drawn to God rather than the accused.

There is no record of what Jesus writes, but someone has suggested that what He writes is familiar to the watching men. Perhaps it is the original Ten Commandments given by God to Moses which include not only adultery as a sin against God but idolatry, murder, theft, lying, slander and greed. We can only guess what Jesus writes with his finger, but His silence and what He writes clearly has an effect on the men who are watching him.

Even so, they keep questioning Him. They want Him to say something and finally, He does. Jesus straightens up and addresses the men first, again drawing eyes away from the accused woman. "Let him who is without sin among you be the first to throw a stone at her," He says and then stoops down again to write on the ground (John 8:7). Just that. Nothing more. Now the accusers are silent. We don't know how long it takes, but John writes that they begin to go away one by one. The older ones leave first, giving truth to the observation that with age comes a measure of humility. Finally, each accuser is gone, and Jesus is left with the woman and the watching crowd.

Something strikes me in this God-encounter between Jesus and the accusers. I understand that He extends grace to them as well as to the woman. In a superficial reading of the account, I easily condemn the men who brought the woman to Jesus. I think, "What's wrong with this picture? It takes two to commit adultery, you know. Where is the man?" I focus on the woman as the victim and see her accusers as the bad guys whom Jesus is teaching a lesson. I see their humiliation and am glad for it.

Yet as I look more deeply into the scene, I realize that Jesus could have humiliated them much more than He did. In fact, He was not humiliating them at all but was extending grace to them as well. Being God, Jesus knew what was in the heart of each man. He could easily have said to one, "Simeon, I know how you cheated on the poor woman who bought meat from you last week," making a public display of Simeon's dishonesty in business. Or He could have said to another, "Matthias, I know how you have been looking at your neighbor's wife for the past month," publicly exposing Matthias' adulterous thoughts. Or again, "Jonas, I hear the lies you say to protect yourself from the criticism of others," revealing Jonas's disobedience to one of God's specific commands.

Jesus knew what was in the heart of each man. He knew that they made choices every day which dishonored God, yet He did not publicly expose their sin. Instead of exposure, He gave an opportunity for honesty and repentance. Jesus challenged each man to face the truth about his life before God, but He did so with grace.

The second God-encounter occurs between the woman and Jesus. She has been watching Him all along, of course, and has seen how Jesus has challenged the men who accused her. She might be wondering if she's "off the hook" or she may simply be waiting for the condemnation she knows she deserves from such a holy man. But when Jesus turns toward her, there is the same look in His eyes, a look full of grace and truth. Jesus does not condemn her, but neither does He condone the way she lives. Grace is different from tolerance, and we see this difference in Jesus' words. He does not say, "Go ahead with your life as it is. You have a right to live any way you want to live and they were wrong to accuse you." He does say, "I do not condemn you. Go now and leave your life of sin" (see John 8:11, paraphrased).

Grace does not condemn while truth declares the way to live. Both are examples of God-love, and both are expressed in Jesus' words. By declaring truth to the woman caught in adultery, Jesus shows that His love is real. Real love will not tolerate the destructive path she is on. It will not let her continue seeking love and fulfilment in unhealthy ways. It will not let her remain in a way of life that is not only destructive for her now but also leads to destruction for eternity. Jesus cares that she becomes the woman she is meant to be and cares enough to tell her how.

Everyone involved in this story was changed when they encountered the real God. I believe that the woman brought before Jesus became one of the most grace-filled women in her town. She had been caught in what was an undeniable sin but had received mercy. She had looked into the eyes of God and seen no condemnation for what she had done, but she had also seen a commitment to how she was to live. She heard in the words of Jesus that grace was real but was only the beginning of change. She was to live differently now.

I believe that she did live differently from that point on, not from a desire to fulfill an impersonal law but from a desire to please a newly personal God. I like to imagine that she became a life-giving person in her community, bringing others into their own God-encounters as they watched a life which now reflected both His grace and truth.

I believe the men who accused and exposed her were also changed by their encounter with the real God. They were challenged to face the truth about their own lives, but the challenge was done in a gracious way. Perhaps they too sensed in Jesus' actions and words a compassion and commitment which reached out to them as much as to the woman they had brought before Him. This may be using too much imagination as I reflect on the account, but I imagine that grace and truth moved them from a righteousness based on outward behavior to one based on purity of heart and mind. I imagine and hope that some of them at least became men who held to God's truth with integrity and taught God's truth with humility and grace.

Another person involved in the story is the modern disciple who reads it in a modern-day Bible. The real you and the real me meet the real God as we see Jesus in action. It occurs to us as we read this story that we are also the woman caught in adultery. We too have chosen a self-life over the God-life we are designed to live. Her choice happened to be adultery, and she happened to get caught. Our choices may be different but they are equally a choice of self-focused life over God-focused life. Our self-focus can be reflected in a prideful or covetous spirit. It can be a quickness to judge, a pursuit of self-glory at the expense of someone else's recognition, a tendency to lie to protect our image or web search that is not good for the soul. It can be any number of things which are not God's design for our life, yet every day we choose them over God.

When Jesus says to the woman, "Go, and from now on sin no more." He uses a strong form of the Greek word for sin. He says to her clearly and emphatically, "Leave this life of sin." The word for sin itself has a meaning in Greek that conveys the idea of an arrow missing a mark.[3] When the woman brought before Jesus heard this word, she understood that He was saying she had been missing the mark in the way she was living. She was meant to aim for something more.

I know that I miss the mark in my relationship with God every day. On a daily basis I miss the mark in the way He has designed me to relate to other people and to respond to life. I might begin every day with time in God's Word and in prayer and leave the house ready to love my neighbors as I know He wants me to, yet the minute I exit the door and encounter a real neighbor, not just an ideal one, I miss the mark. Loving is easy when I'm alone. Living to please God is possible when life goes my way and nothing happens to dampen my spirits. But throw a few challenging people and one or two upsetting circumstances into the day, and I realize how much grace and truth are still lacking in my soul.

Thankfully, even as daily I miss the mark, I continually receive grace from the One who is grace to the core of His being. When I live in awareness of how much grace I receive from God every day, I can become a person of grace who says, "I, who sin all the time, receive grace from God every day. Because I've received so much grace, I can give it to you." And as daily I learn to walk in His truth, I can also become a person of truth who says, "There is a way that leads to life and we can walk with God in it."

Hope in the process

I am hopeful as I read through the Gospels and watch the real God in action. I hear Jesus teach and watch Him interact with people who are just like me—people like Nicodemus who long for something deeper than what they currently experience of God, like the men who are blind to the log in their own eye, like the adulterous woman who gets life wrong and needs someone to show her how to get it right—and I see people who change. I am glad that Jesus shows grace because I need it so much in my own life. But I am equally glad that it is grace He shows and not tolerance, because I need truth spoken into my life as well.

When God does not hesitate to show me where I am wrong in the way I think and live, this assures me that He cares. John of the Cross wrote centuries ago, "Let us suffice to say, then, that God perceives the imperfections within us, and because of his love for us, urges us to grow up."[4] I am glad that God does not hesitate to speak truth into my life and wants me to grow up. I am glad that He wants me to return to my "true self," become all I am meant to be. and does not hesitate to speak truth into my life. It gives me real hope for real change.

I am equally glad that Jesus reveals grace since I am daily aware of my inability to honor God in the way I live, and lest someone reading this should immediately wonder if I suffer from low self-esteem, I can only say that the actual problem is more of too-high a self-esteem. I am daily aware of the self and its clinging cousins which lurk in the well of my soul. Self -focus, self-promotion, self-protection, self-defense— and the list goes on—are alive and well.

God is aware of this, too, and His grace gives me hope in the process. I take comfort in the words that God spoke to the apostle Paul when he was feeling keenly a personal weakness and was longing for it to change. "My grace is sufficient for you, for my power is made perfect in weakness" (2 Cor. 12:9). God has not left us to live the Christian life on our own. His power is available, and our weakness is not a problem for Him.

C. S. Lewis reminds us in *Mere Christianity* that "We need not despair even in our worst, for our failures are forgiven. The only fatal thing is to sit down content with anything less than perfection."[5] Centuries earlier François Fénelon gave this counsel to a friend who was frustrated with obvious and continual weaknesses: "Despair of yourself as much as you please, but not of God."[6] Lewis tells us to put our failures in their proper place and not let them keep us from pursuing holiness. Fénelon reminds us to focus more on God than on our weakness. It all boils down to this. We belong to a God who is both grace and truth. We are to pursue living by His truth but at the same time, we can rest in His grace.

REAL LIFE WITH A REAL GOD

"Bear with yourself, avoiding both self-deception and discouragement. This is a medium rarely attained. People either look complacently on themselves and their good intentions, or they despair utterly. Expect nothing of yourself, but all things of God. Knowledge of our own hopeless, incorrigible weakness, with unreserved confidence in God's power are the true foundations of all spiritual life." –François Fénelon[7]

1. Read the God-encounter in John 8:2–11 and put yourself in the story. Imagine yourself as one of Jesus' disciples, one of the people in the crowd, the woman caught in adultery, one of the men who brings her to Jesus. What do you think of Jesus' response to the accusers? To the woman? Pay attention to how you feel about each of these responses.

2. Which is needed at this time in your life with God, a more intentional pursuit of holiness or a greater awareness of grace?

3. Talk with God about what rises up within your soul as you read this account. Then reflect on this poem by George Herbert.[8] Let it lead you to an honest conversation with God.

> Love bade me welcome; yet my soul drew back,
> Guilty of dust and sin.
> But quick-eyed Love, observing me grow slack
> From my first entrance in,
> Drew nearer to me, sweetly questioning
> If I lack'd anything.

"A guest," I answer'd, "worthy to be here."
Love said, "You shall be he."
"I, the unkind, ungrateful? Ah, my dear,
I cannot look on Thee."
Love took my hand and smiling did reply,
"Who made the eyes but I?"
"Truth, Lord; but I have marr'd them: let my shame
Go where it doth deserve."
"And know you not," says Love, "Who bore the blame?"
"My dear, then I will serve."
"You must sit down," says Love, "and taste my meat."
So I did sit and eat.

8

A Divine Exchange

By his first work he gave me to myself; and by the next he gave himself to me. And when he gave himself, he gave me back myself that I had lost.–Bernard of Clairvaux[1]

Therefore, if anyone is in Christ, he is a new creation. The old has passed away; behold, the new has come. All this is from God, who through Christ reconciled us to himself. (2 Cor. 5:17–18)

Belonging to God, believing Him and bearing His image are what we are made for, but we cannot be who we are meant to be. We cannot live from our God-given places of deepest significance, deepest security and deepest satisfaction. The Great Handover and sin's entrance in the world took care of that. Thankfully, God loved us too much to let the Great Handover be our final human condition. His pursuing love and Christ's sacrificial death on the cross took care of sin and made it possible for our souls to come home. We are once more where we belong, once more believing what is true and able to live as we are meant to live.

When a friend of mine from post-university years understood this and began to live in the truth and grace of Christ, there was joy and celebration. Glenn understood and thought it was great that the angels in heaven rejoiced that his soul had found its way home. There was also genuine joy in his heart. "I once was lost but now I'm found, was blind but now I see," he was fond of saying to anyone who would listen.

Out of joy and thankfulness for what was done for him, Glenn began an earnest effort to live for God. He began to read the Bible on a regular basis, joined a prayer group and considered church a place for service, not just membership. "We go to church not to get something out of it, but to give to it," was something Glenn picked up along the way, and he was fond of saying it. He sincerely wanted to be a witness for Christ and made an effort to be nicer to the people in his office especially the boss who, he admitted, made his life fairly miserable from Monday through Friday.

Although we both lived in the same city, Glenn and I did not attend the same church. Busy with our respective jobs, we did not see each other that often, but one day we connected by scheduling time for coffee in a small café near his office. As we caught up on each other's lives, I was a little surprised to see how subdued he became when the conversation touched on spiritual matters. In particular, I had asked how things were going at work.

"It's not working," Glenn said. "I can't do this love thing. Being patient doesn't come easy to me, you know. And don't talk about loving my boss. I used to say I'll love anyone God wants me to love even if it kills me. Remember that? Now I'm pretty sure it's going to."

I asked how things were going at church. "Oh, that too," he responded. "I'm glad to be involved and all, but lately it seems like 'just a lot of busy,' if you know what I mean. I thought I would be at least a little more different by now, more loving, more patient, more like Jesus. But even some people at church get me going. I'm ashamed sometimes of the way I react." He paused before adding, "I thought I'd be changed by now. Sometimes I just don't think I have it in me to love." He must have seen my concerned expression, because he added quickly and with an obvious effort to be positive, "Don't worry about me. No one knows I feel this way at church. I'm on the worship team and still enjoy it. I won't give up. Love God and love people, you know. That's what it's all about."

My friend was obviously discouraged and it seemed his discouragement centered on his efforts to live for Christ. Glenn was involved in church; he was seeking to live for Christ, but had lost joy of life *with* Christ in the effort. He was especially discouraged when he saw how little he had changed over time. In trying to reflect Christ at work, he could only see what a poor reflection he was no matter how hard he tried to be different.

In a December issue of *Good Housekeeping* magazine, the editor-in-chief, Rosemary Ellis, reflected on what the Christmas holidays do to our joy. "I love December," she wrote, "but it is fraught with so many expectations and obligations—both real and self-imposed—that I invariably end up feeling overwhelmed and exhausted by the end of the holidays." One feels, she concludes, "that the work has overtaken the celebration."[2] This is perhaps what happened to Glenn. The work was overtaking the celebration.

I also heard some image-projection in our conversation. Glenn felt a need to hide what he was feeling in church because he was on a worship team. He felt a need to hide from me the depth of his discouragement. He wanted to assure me that he was doing okay and would keep "loving God and loving people" even though it was obvious that both were an area of struggle.

Image-projection has a way of creeping into the Christian life and into the church. I know this from experience. It took some time for me to realize that as sincerely as I was trying to live for Christ, life was still more about me than about the One I was so diligently trying to serve. It was about me living for God, me trying to be a better Christian, me trying to produce patience, compassion and kindness, and display peace and self-control; in other words, my life was not so much about Christ but about me trying to be and do all the things I had learned one must be and do as a Christian. Like Glenn, my faith was real and so was my desire to live for Christ, yet trying to live for Him produced more effort than rest. Imagine a tree without roots straining hard to produce fruit, and you get the picture.

Over time I too began to live less by the celebration and more by the expectations and obligations—real and self-imposed, and most often self-imposed. Eventually, thanks to God's mercy on a sincere but struggling saint, I began to understand that my efforts to live well for Christ were rooted in a limited understanding of His work on the cross. Like Glenn, I had rightly understood that Jesus' sacrificial death gave me a new status with God. Once I was lost, now I am found. Once I was dead in my sins, now I am alive. Once I was separated from God, now I have a relationship with God. There was much to celebrate for what Christ had done for me. The problem was that I thought of the celebration as a party at the foot of the cross. Beyond the cross, there was work to be done and I was the one to do it. Eventually, I too began to feel the exhaustion of trying to live for Christ and trying to be like Him. I just didn't have it in me.

I remember well an evening of conversation with God about a year after I had given my life to Christ. I was talking with Him about my frustrations. There was no doubt some "poor me" in the conversation, but there was also a sincere desire to honor Him in the way it was lived. "I'm trying to live for You, Lord. I'm trying to be like You, but I'm more aware now of how hard this is than I was a year ago when I gave You my life. You say to love as You have loved me. I really want to, but it's a tall order, and I can't seem to do it no matter how hard I try."

"You're right," God responded in the quiet but firm way that I've come to know as His voice. "You can't do it, no matter how hard you try. And that's why I came. You know what My death on the cross means for you. Now I want to teach you what My resurrected life means. Understand what it means that I am a Living Presence in your life, and you'll begin to see real change."

"I don't have it in me"

Loving God with all our heart, soul, mind and strength and loving others as Jesus has loved us is the way we are meant to live, but God has not left us alone in the effort. The Father reminded me of this early in our life together, and this revelation changed the way I lived for Him as well as with Him. This truth came back to me as Glenn and I talked together in the coffee shop, and so I shared with him what I had heard from the Father some years before. "You're right, Glenn, you don't have it in you. That's why Jesus came." I also suggested to Glenn that he should be encouraged that he was struggling with real life for God. This means it mattered to him. It was also evidence that it mattered to God and God was using Glenn's dissatisfaction to get his attention.

Jesus came to make possible our life with God but also to make possible our life for God as a reflection of His image in the world. Beyond the cross, Jesus is alive and He takes up residence in every soul that claims Him as Savior and Lord. This is a profound biblical truth. The Great Handover which led to the Great Cover-Up has now become the Great Restoration. Only the One who is Himself the image of God can restore God's image in us.

I am meant to bear God's image, not project my own. Not even my own image as a good Christian. The truth that only Christ can produce His character in me is incredibly freeing. It frees me from one of the most clinging cousins of the self-life, which is self-effort. And clinging to the heels of self-effort is often two other cousins of the "Self Clan," an inward-focused self-pity and outward-focused self-protection, because we feel deficient in our efforts and try to hide the deficiencies from those around us. Working for Christ outwardly without remaining connected to Him inwardly leads to a performance-oriented Christianity. Self-effort leaves Christ at the cross while I live the Christian life. But Christ is not still on the cross. Salvation from sin and redemption from Satan's death-producing control is only the beginning of His work. Restoration as an image-bearer is the work of Christ after the cross. A risen Christ living in me through the transforming power of the Spirit and revealing Himself through me to a broken world is a vital part of God's story of redemption and restoration.

Unless I believe this, however, I continue to miss a vital truth about the Christian life. Self-effort keeps me from resting in what Christ has accomplished. Celebration becomes work. Grace becomes law once again. And I am right where the enemy of the soul wants me; saved from sin, yes, but still living apart from God. Satan may not have me for eternity (Christ's work on the cross has taken care of that), but he keeps me from the fullness of life that God intends for me here.

It all boils down to this. "In Christ alone my hope is found,"[3] not only for redemption but for restoration.

All that He is became ours

How is such restoration possible? Sylvia Gunter explains it in this way, "A divine exchange took place when we made a new covenant with our heavenly Father through confession of our faith in Jesus. He gave us his character, his name, his nature, his essence represented by all his names. All that he is became ours."[4] This is good news indeed. Image-bearing is possible because the gospel message includes a liberating truth: "Christ in you, the hope of glory" (Col. 1:27). Scripture makes it clear that Christ is the image of God and that He lives in us.

> *Christ is the image of God*: "He is the image of the invisible God, the firstborn of all creation." "He [the Son] is the radiance of the glory of God and the exact imprint of his nature." "The god of this world has blinded the minds of the unbelievers, to keep them from seeing the light of the gospel of the glory of Christ, who is the image of God." (Col. 1:15; Heb. 1:3; 2 Cor. 4:4)

Christ dwells in us: "If anyone loves me, he will keep my word, and my Father will love him, and we will come to him and make our home with him." "Whoever abides in me and I in him, he it is that bears much fruit. . . ." "so that Christ may dwell in your hearts through faith..." "For in him [Christ] the whole fullness of deity dwells bodily, and you have been filled in him, who is the head of all rule and authority." (John 14:23; John 15:5; Eph. 3:17; Col. 2:9–10)

To be in Christ is to be a new creation: "Therefore, if anyone is in Christ, he is a new creation. The old has passed away; behold, the new has come." "We were buried therefore with him by baptism into death, in order that, just as Christ was raised from the dead by the glory of the Father, we too might walk in newness of life." ". . . and to be renewed in the spirit of your minds, and to put on the new self, created after the likeness of God in true righteousness and holiness." (2 Cor. 5:17; Rom. 6:4; Eph. 4:23–24)

We are being transformed into the likeness of Christ: "And we all, with unveiled face, beholding the glory of the Lord, are being transformed into the same image from one degree of glory to another. For this comes from the Lord who is the Spirit." "Just as we have borne the image of the man of dust, we shall also bear the image of the man of heaven." "For those whom he foreknew he also predestined to be conformed to the image of his Son." (2 Cor. 3:18; 1 Cor. 15:49; Rom. 8:29)

The New Testament letters confirm the centrality of Christ and His transforming presence in the church. Paul defines spiritual maturity to the Ephesian church asattaining "to the measure of the stature of the fullness of Christ" (Eph.

4:13). He tells the church in Colossae that a goal of ministry is to "present everyone mature in Christ" (Col. 1:28). In fact, the entire letter to the Colossians is an exaltation of Christ in both the community life of the church and personal life of the believer. Would that every church in the world today would make a scuba diving expedition into the book of Colossians to plumb its depths and let the Spirit work its life-giving truths into the life of the church.

Paul's letter to the Colossians reveals the centrality of Christ in the church, but it is in his letter to the Galatian Christians where we find a key to the centrality of Christ as individuals. We can even find elements of designer living in Paul's words to the Galatians:

I have been crucified with Christ. It is no longer I who live, but Christ who lives in me. And the life I now live in the flesh I live by faith in the Son of God, who loved me and gave himself for me. (2:20)

I have come to view Galatians 2:20 as Paul's instructions to the church on designer living. In this verse we find three designer elements: a designer image, designer logo and designer slogan.

Designer living

A *designer image* is the signature "look" of a product. We can tell by a glance if a shoe or pocketbook is made by a style-conscious designer from Europe or an earth-conscious designer from Middle America. Not only fashion but household products, computers and iPhones, furniture and cars can often tell us at a glance the store where they were purchased or the company that made them. The Christian, according to Paul, also has a signature "look." Our designer image is "Christ who lives in me" (Gal. 2:20). When people see us, they should be able to say, "There goes a Christian," or at least wonder if we are Christians because of the way we act and speak. What they see in our lives and what they hear in our voices should reflect a living and indwelling Christ.

Growth for the Christian is growth in Christlikeness. As a Christian matures spiritually, he begins to think less of himself and more of Christ. He begins to think of his reputation in the eyes of others only as it relates to the reputation of the Christ he reveals to the people who cross his path each day: his coworkers in the office, the clerk behind the counter, his wife and children at home. He speaks less about what he is doing and more about what God is doing. His choices are increasingly shaped by a desire to honor and reflect Christ. Relationships are increasingly shaped by the love of Christ that is growing within a soul more and more conformed to the image of Christ. He is beginning to look like the One who made him, redeemed him and is transforming him.

We are also familiar with *designer logos*. A flowing check on a t-shirt is designed to make one think of sports. The logo reveals the focus of the company that makes these products. It also brings expectations of quality. The same applies for any electronic device which displays an apple with a bite out of it. When see this logo on a product, we know immediately the company which produced it and expect quality if we buy it.

Our designer logo, writes Paul, is the cross. We are "crucified with Christ," he writes, and the cross is a key to our new life. 2:20)The one-time work of the cross is our hope of salvation; the ongoing work of the cross is our hope of restoration. Whenever we see a cross rising high above the roof of a building or dangling on a piece of jewelry, we immediately connect the building or the person with Christianity. Such a connection means something in our minds and it produces expectations. It means redemption and restoration is happening in this place and in this life. It means we expect Christ-honoring and Christ-life in this person or this place. We may be disappointed in our expectations, but nonetheless, the expectation is there and has a right to be. No matter how imperfect is the person or place which displays a cross, the cross itself represents a divine focus and a divine quality to a watching world.

Designer slogans are also familiar to us. Of course, a familiarity with slogans depends on one's personal passions. A sports fan can immediately tie the words "Just do it" to Nike, "I am what I am" to Reebok and "Impossible is nothing" to Adidas. If someone's passion is cars, they might agree that "There is no substitute" for a Porsche even if they can't afford to own one themselves.

While the designer logo is visual and brings instant recognition to the eyes and an immediate connection to the company behind the product, a designer slogan is mental. It is created to plant an idea in the mind that suggests something about the product itself.

Advertising experts will tell us that a slogan must have certain elements to be effective. Among these elements are consistency, identification and distinction. A good slogan is consistent with what it represents; otherwise the words will be meaningless. No one will identify the words with the product. Even more detrimental is when a product does not meet up to the expectations produced by a slogan. There is a good chance that people will discount the product itself and even more damaging, distrust the company which produced it, which is definitely not what a company wants to happen. Consistency is important because it influences identification. Distinction happens when an effective slogan sets the product apart from everything else that is on the market.

Paul gives a designer slogan that captures the essence of a Christian's distinctive identity in the world and gives a key to living consistently as image-bearers.

"No longer I, but Christ" (see Gal. 2:20)

These five words, short and simple, capture what it means to live as a Christian. They state what sets us apart from the crowd, and guide us on the road to Christlikeness.

There are other words which capture elements of the Christian life such as "Christ in you the hope of glory" (Col. 1:27) and "count it all joy" (James 1:2) and "for me to live is Christ" (Phil. 1:21). These phrases come from Scripture and all are meant for more than clever Sunday school choruses. They state profound biblical truths and are helpful in thinking correctly as we grow as Christians. But five simple words, "No longer I, but Christ" give the key to real change. These words and the truth behind them liberate us from thinking that Christlikeness happens by self-effort. They lead us to the truth that Christ-the image of-God, lives in me and lives through me.

What are the liberating differences between the old way of thinking tied to self-effort and the new way of "no longer I, but Christ"? The old way emphasizes what I do (image-projection) while the new way emphasizes what God does (Christ in me: image-bearing). The old way draws from my resources (self-focus), while the new draws from God's resources (God-focus). The old lives from the outside in (modifying the way I behave without changing the way I think) while the new lives from the inside out (changing the way I think so that how I act flows from a truly transformed life).

This truth of an indwelling Christ has not only been liberating but has brought more real change in my life than I've ever known as a Christian. It began with death to self, including the self that wanted to be a good Christian but was trying to do so by its own effort. I nailed my "false self"—with its concern for the opinions of others, its self-focused efforts to live for Christ, its self-referenced way of looking at people and responding to circumstances—nailed it to the cross. I moved self with all of its clinging cousins out of the way so that Jesus could have His way in me. At this point, real change began, and I began to move toward the life I was created to live.

Did I change in a moment, in the blinking of an eye? I wish! I would love for God to have zapped me into a perfect outward expression of this newly learned truth. Alas, He did not. But He started me on the journey to wholeness and He gave me a promise for the journey: "He who began a good work in you will bring it to completion at the day of Jesus Christ" (Phil. 1:6).

This is good news for everyone who desires to honor Christ but is faced daily with the sin and self which still influence the way we live. It is good news for the new Christian sitting in the back row on the left side of the sanctuary every Sunday, singing about God's love while thinking he can't love some of the students in his class, not the way they act toward him. It is good news for the man who is serving communion, walking slowly down the aisle and carefully avoiding the eyes of two people he recently offended with angry comments. It is good news for the ones he offended as they struggle to forgive him. It is good news for the woman in the third row on the right who sincerely wants to be patient and kind but cannot keep irritation and resentment inside whenever she talks with a coworker in the office no matter how hard she tries. It is good news for the husband struggling with a pull toward pornography even after ten years of a good marriage. It is good news for all who sincerely long to live as God has designed us to live. He intends for us to become conformed to His image and is Himself at work to make it happen.

I want to make it clear that in focusing on the truth of God's transforming work in us through Christ, I am not saying that we never seek help elsewhere in the change process. God is committed to our restoration and, in the journey toward wholeness and freedom, He often provides help along the way. Sometimes the helper is a friend with whom we can be honest about our struggles and who will pray with us without judgment. Such a friend is a gift from God.

As Glenn and I talked in the coffee shop about the hope-giving reality of the Christ-life already in us, I encouraged him to ask God for such a friend. It might be someone in his worship team or small-group Bible study. It might be a friend outside of his church, or someone trained in spiritual direction, but it would be someone who would journey with him as he sought a deeper experience of God and real change.

Sometimes we need professional help in the change process. Wholeness in Christ is not just spiritual wholeness, but emotional and mental as well. When we enter new life in Christ, we come with all that has shaped us to the point of new life. Family history, life experience, relational experience, personality, culture—all of these shape us deeply and not always in healthy ways. We enter new life in Christ with patterns of thinking and ways of relating that are so deeply ingrained that we are often not aware of their presence. Nor do we recognize their influence on our current struggles. Psychiatrists, psychologists and counselors are trained to recognize mental health issues as well as unhealthy patterns of thinking and relating. They have professional understanding of how people change which is invaluable in our movement toward wholeness. Seeking the help of a professional does not deny healing that comes from the indwelling presence of Christ. It recognizes professional counseling and treatment as instruments of His healing.

God provides help along the way and companions on the journey. He gives soul-encouragement through friendship and soul-help through professional counseling or spiritual direction. Each of these is a life-giving instrument in His hands and can lead us toward wholeness as image-bearers. But we must also take hold of the truth that Christ is our hope and Christ in us is a reality. This is not merely a message to hear in church but a truth to apply in every place and every day of life as Kenneth Boa reminds us in *Conformed to His Image*:

> Jesus summed it up this way in these simple but profound words in John 14:20: 'you in Me, and I in you.' The 'you in me' refers to our relationship with Christ by virtue of our life in him. The 'I in you' speaks of our fellowship with Christ by virtue of his life in us. . . . As we abide in Christ, his life in us can qualitatively affect every aspect of our earthly existence.[5]

We see the Christ instead

We are meant to be image-bearers and are unable to be so on our own, although we make a good effort at image-projection even as Christians. God alone can restore His image in us, and He has done this through Christ's work on the cross. An indwelling Christ and a transforming Holy Spirit makes image-bearing possible once again. What happens when the real you meets the real God? Real change. The kind of change that brings integrity of life as who we are on the outside flows from who we are on the inside. The kind of change that makes us whole again and free.

A poem by Beatrice Cleland, which bears the title *Indwelt*, captures beautifully what designer living can look like in a person. It is written as the voice of someone who knows a Christian and sees in him or her a designer image. The person she addresses might be anyone, a friend or family member, a coworker or even a stranger she encounters in an elevator. Could it be said of you? Could it be said of me?

> Not merely in the words you say,
> Not only in your deeds confessed,
> But in the most unconscious way,
> Is Christ through you expressed.
> Is it just a beatific smile,
> A holy light upon your brow?
> Oh no, I felt His presence
> When you laughed just now.
> For me 'twas not the truth you taught
> To you so clear, to me so dim,
> But when you came to see me,
> You brought a sense of Him.
> And from your eyes He beckons me,

And from your heart His love is shed,
Till I lose sight of you
And see the Christ instead.[6]

Real Life with a Real God:

"Think of the wonder of it all—the Fountain of Life Himself wells up within us, taking the place of all that we have delivered bit by bit, into His grave. 'I live, yet not I, but Christ liveth in me.' Little have we proved, any of us, the resources that lie in that mighty indwelling, little have we learned what it is to have all our soul-fibers penetrated by its power. May God lead us, no matter what the cost, into all that *can* be known of it, here on earth."–Lilias Trotter[7]

1. Spend time with God in His Word and reflect on the following truths:
   - Christ the image of God: Col. 1:15; Heb. 1:3; 2 Cor. 4:4
   - Christ dwells in us: John 14:23; John 15:5; Eph. 3:17; Col. 2:9–10
   - To be in Christ is to be a new creation: 2 Cor. 5:17; Rom. 6:4; Eph. 4:23
   - We are being transformed into the image of Christ: 2 Cor. 3:18; 1 Cor. 15:49; Rom. 8:29

2. Read the following verses and ask for each one: Do I really believe this? What difference should it make in the way I think about myself; in the way I live?
   Col. 1:22   Gal. 2:20–21   1 Pet. 1:3–4

3. Reflect on the three elements of designer living found in Gal. 2:20. How can you apply this in your life?

- Designer image: Christ who lives in me
- Designer logo: the cross
- Designer slogan: No longer I, but Christ

4. Real change comes when we meet the real God. We meet Him in Jesus and we learn that transformation happens as the Spirit conforms us to His image. Talk with God about these truths and how you can live them more fully.

9

A Greater Yes

I like Jesus but I'm not so sure that I want to be like Him."

George approached us and spoke these words on the last day of a summer series on spiritual formation which Louis and I had been teaching. He was in his sixties at the time of the class, and it may well be that he had attended the class not so much to grow in his spiritual life but to hear from the missionaries his church had been supporting for some time. Certainly, he had not expected to be challenged as a Christian.

George assured us that his faith in Christ was an important part of his life. He believed the Christian life was the right way for him to live, as opposed to the Buddhist, Muslim, Hindu, new age, humanist, atheist or any number of other possible ways to live. As a Christian, George understood that the church has some claim to his time and money and sought to be faithful in these commitments. But now he was hearing that Jesus Himself had a claim on his life, not as a distant God to believe in and celebrate twice a year at Christmas and Easter, but as a real and present Lord to know and follow and be changed by. Previously spiritual formation meant little more to George than attending a Sunday school class and growing in knowledge of the Bible. Now he understood it to mean growing in likeness to Christ. His thought life, his actions and reactions, his attitudes and habits, how he felt about himself on any given day, how he did business and how he related to others—all were to be conformed to the image of Christ. This was more than he had realized it meant to be a Christian. It needed some reflection.

Dietrich Bonhoeffer touches on George's understanding of the Christian life in his book, *The Cost of Discipleship*. Bonhoeffer's words are well-known and often quoted as a call to serious discipleship, yet what he calls "abstract theology" and "general religious knowledge" still prevail in many churches today:

> When we are called to follow Christ, we are summoned to an exclusive attachment to his person. . . . Discipleship means adherence to Christ. . . . An abstract Christology, a doctrinal system, a general religious knowledge on the subject of grace or on the forgiveness of sins, render discipleship superfluous. . . . With an abstract idea it is possible to enter into a relation of formal knowledge, to become enthusiastic about it, and perhaps even to put it into practice; but it can never be followed in personal obedience.[2]

We were glad that George approached us with this honest remark. It meant that he had been listening and had felt something stirring within, even if it made him uncomfortable. Abstract theology and general religious knowledge,

even about Jesus, is not discipleship. We are called to follow a Person, Bonhoeffer reminds us, and this Person is to
become our deepest attachment. George realized that up to
this point he had been attached to the Christian way of life,
yet not really attached to Christ. An attachment to Jesus
would touch his life in new ways, and he would be changed
by it. Did he want to change so deeply?

Real desire

Real change, as anyone who has abandoned countless
New Year resolutions can affirm, begins with real desire. By
"real desire" I mean a desire so fundamental, so deep, that it
determines the choices we make, even our spontaneous ones,
as opposed to countless surface desires that change umpteen
times a day depending on how we feel at any given moment.
One may, for example, desire to lose weight yet a moment of
choice in a restaurant may result in ordering the molten lava
cake whose picture stares so invitingly from a menu. I know
about this, having been at this moment of decision countless
times—and having chosen cake. The desire to lose weight is
real but is obviously not deep enough to say "no" to a more
immediate and inviting desire.

If, however, we are diagnosed with diabetes and realize
with some shock how seriously our health is jeopardized by
what we eat, we begin to think differently about even a piece
of chocolate cake. No matter how inviting and available it
is to us, there is something we now value more than the
cake. We place greater value on our health now and begin
to focus on a healthier lifestyle. At first, the cake is still a
temptation, but with practice and time, we no longer have
to grit our teeth and steel our emotions against such a sweet

offering. The offering and others like it remain on the menu, but they have less appeal. An increasing satisfaction with a healthy body exposes chocolate cake for what it is, merely cake, damaging to our health and, even more significant, no longer a necessity for happiness.

Using chocolate cake as an example of temptation is not meant to make light of the struggles that we face daily in remaining true to God's standards in the world today. I give the example to make a key point about change. No matter what we say we desire and no matter how sincerely we say we desire it, our choices reveal what we really want. For real change to happen, we must change what we choose and for that we must change what we most desire.

A greater yes

Richard Rolle, one of England's great spiritual leaders in the fourteenth century, observed that "people become like what they love; for they take their tone from the greed of their day and age."[3] Rolle's words were spoken centuries ago but are just as true today. We become like what we love. If we love the spirit of the age, we will increasingly reflect the spirit of the age in our thoughts and words, actions and reactions. If we love Jesus, our thoughts, words, actions and reactions will increasingly reflect this likeness.

This is true for a young man and woman who sincerely want to hold to biblical standards but who are faced with the physical and emotional pull of sexual desire. Something stronger than good intentions to live by sound doctrine is needed to enable them to say "no" to an encounter which is not only desirable but is readily available. Bonhoeffer was right when he noted that one can be enthusiastic about doctrine but one is not inspired to obedience by it. Adherence to a Person one knows and loves and would not want to disappoint inspires obedience more than abstract theology.

A young woman who is growing in a relationship with Jesus discovers that He is as real to her as everyone else in her life. A parent's love and the love of a friend, boyfriend or fiancé may be deep and real, but Jesus's love is deeper still. In fact, it is deeper and more real than any love she will know on earth, even once she marries. Going through each day with Jesus as her closest companion, the young woman begins to value Him more than anything or anyone else. He becomes her "Greater Yes."

A young man has found, in Jesus, someone worth living for and worth following all the way to a personal cross, if Jesus asks it of him. Jesus is becoming as real to him as all the other relationships he enjoys and he wants to honor the One he follows in these relationships, even if he must deny himself to do so. In a moment of choice, the young man chooses to live by Christ's standards, not because they are good standards, but because they are His. Jesus is becoming the Greater Yes who shapes his life and determines his choices, even when following Jesus means walking a road of self-denial and surrender.

Real discipleship

Jesus never implied that following Him would be easy. He taught often and in varied ways on the subject of discipleship and each time made clear what is required for anyone who wants to be His disciple.

If anyone would come after me, let him deny himself and take up his cross daily and follow me. (Luke 9:23)

If anyone comes to me and does not hate his own father and mother and wife and children and brothers and sisters, yes, and even his own life, he cannot be my disciple. (14:26)

So therefore, any one of you who does not renounce all that he has cannot be my disciple. (14:33)

Self-denial. Taking up a cross. Giving up everything we have. Loyalty to Jesus above natural earthly relationships. These are strong conditions. There must have been many in the listening crowd who thought, like George, "Well, Jesus, I like what You do and I like what You say. I even like You. But I'm not sure I want to be like You if this is what it means to be a disciple." When we reflect on the conditions Jesus gives for discipleship, however, we hear in His words a reversal of the Great Handover.

• *Absolute loyalty* over our closest earthly relationships is a reversal of the moment when Adam chose loyalty to Eve or loyalty to God. If Adam had chosen loyalty to God over Eve, she may well have accused him of "hating her." We have a tendency to think this way when people do not agree with us, no matter how right they may be.

• *Absolute surrender* and *denial of self* are a reversal of Eve's and then Adam's choice to reach for something they wanted but which they knew was against their God-designed identity and purpose.

• *Take up the cross daily* is an ongoing reversal of the Great Handover as we practice a voluntary death that gets self out of the way so we be image-bearers once again.

Taking up the cross as a condition of discipleship evoked graphic images to an audience who understood the cross was an instrument of death. It was the equivalent of the guillotine or electric chair. No one would voluntarily choose a cross, especially every day, but this is exactly what Jesus tells us we are to do as His disciples.

What is the cross that we are to take up as we follow Jesus? Sometimes we equate the cross we bear to something or someone outside of ourselves and reduce its meaning to a challenging relationship or a difficult situation we have to endure. "I guess my coworker is just the cross I have to bear," we say with a sigh. "This illness of yours is certainly a cross Jesus is asking you to bear," we tell a friend with sincere sympathy but a misguided interpretation of Jesus' words. Robert Mulholland in his book *Invitation to a Journey* gives a much more clear interpretation of the cross that Jesus tells us to take up on a daily basis, and I have emphasized his main point with italics to make sure we don't miss this vital truth:

> Our cross is not the cantankerous person we have to deal with day by day. Our cross is not the employer we just can't get along with. Our cross is not the neighbor or work colleague who cuts across the grain in every single time of relationship. Nor is our cross the difficulties and infirmities that the flow of life brings to us beyond our control. *Our cross is the point of our unlikeness to the image of Christ*, where we must die to self in order to be raised by God into wholeness of life in the image of Christ right there at that point . . . the process of being conformed to the image of Christ takes place at the points of our unlikeness to Christ.[4]

What does it mean practically to take up the cross daily? It means that I voluntarily die every day to the places where I am unlike Christ. I willingly crucify the self-life that hinders the Christ-life which is necessary to my becoming an image-bearer once again. Self-defensiveness and self-promotion, self-righteousness and self-pity, self-focus and self-serving, whatever remains alive of the "I" which exists apart from Christ in the way I think and speak, act and react—all need to die in the moment I become aware of them. Jesus commands a loyalty from those who follow Him so complete that we willingly die to self in order to live for Him. This, too, is a reversal of the moment when Eve chose her way, which was really Satan's way, over God's way.

If anyone has a right to demand absolute loyalty, obedience and surrender, it is the One who gave everything for us. Jesus was willing to do whatever was necessary to bring redemption and restoration to our souls. It took everything He had to offer . . . all of Himself in obedience nailed to a cross.

"Our Lord demands all," wrote Amy Carmichael, as she reflected on His conditions of discipleship. "I see nothing less in His words about taking up a cross. It is all or nothing. I don't mean that one sees all there is to see at first, or even at last, but only that all we know is given because we want to give all. And faith shall sing a joyous Yes to every dear command of Thine. He poured out all for us. Can we measure our offering to Him?"[5]

Whatever it takes

When we were university students in the late 1970s, Louis and I had the privilege of hearing Dr. Helen Rose-veare speak of her experiences as a missionary doctor in the Democratic Republic of the Congo. The title of her message was "The Cost of Obedience." As Dr. Roseveare stood on the platform, she was holding on to what appeared to be a tall branch with flowering leaves projecting on all sides. As she began her message, she slowly stripped the leaves from the branch. She spoke of how the children in the village would do the same to branches they found in the forest. What were they making, she asked, as they tore the leaves and flowers, ruthlessly stripping away everything that defined the plant and made it beautiful? Eventually, Dr. Roseverare stopped pulling and tearing at the branch and we could see what she held in her hand. It was an arrow.

To the students watching in the audience, myself included, her illustration was a powerful visual image of the transforming work of Christ. The image remains in my mind even today. Some years later my husband and I were preparing for ministry in Africa with WEC International, the same mission as Dr. Roseveare, and we began to read her books. In one of them, we discovered a reference to this visual image which had impacted us as students. Her words once again challenged us. George would have appreciated them, too, since they contain her own honest questions:

> To be thus transformed, was I willing—am I still willing—for the whittling, sandpapering, stripping, processes necessary in my Christian life?

> The ruthless pulling off of leaves and flowers might include doing without a television set or washing machine, remaining single in order to see a job done, re-evaluating the worthiness of the ambition to be a "good" doctor (according to my terms and values).

The snapping of thorns might include drastic dealing with hidden jealousies and unknown prides, giving up prized rights in leadership and administration. The final stripping of the bark might include lessons to be learned regarding death to self—self-defense, self-pity, self-justi-fication, self-vindication, self-sufficiency, all the mecha-nisms of preventing the hurt of too deep involvement.

Am I prepared for the pain, which may at times seem like sacrifice, in order to be made a tool in His service?[6]

Dr. Roseveare goes on to equate a willingness to change with a Greater Yes to Christ in response to what He has done for her:

My willingness will be a measure of the sincerity of my desire to express my heartfelt gratitude to Him for his so-great salvation. Can I see such minor "sacrifices" in light of the great sacrifice of Calvary, where Christ gave all for me?[7]

One would think that a young family preparing to give up everything they knew to live in unknown places had al-ready answered the question of willingness. And in a way we had answered; in the big ways, at least, such as willingness to give up life in the United States for life in one of the poorest countries in the world. Yet we were still greatly challenged by her words. I remember wondering one Sunday morning as I sang hymns which declared a love for Christ and desire to live wholly for Him, "Do I know what it really means to live wholly for Christ, with nothing held back?" Helen Ros-eveare's words are so true and challenging, that it is worth continuing to quote her, and she has given me permission to quote so extensively:

To love the Lord my God with *all* my soul will involve a spiritual cost. I'll have to give Him my heart, and let Him love through it whom and how He wills, even if this seems at times to break my heart.

To love the Lord my God with *all* my soul will involve a volitional and emotional cost. I'll have to give Him my will, my rights to decide and choose, and all my relationships, for Him to guide and control, even when I cannot understand His reasoning.

To love the Lord my God with *all* my mind will involve an intellectual cost. I must give Him my mind, my intelligence, my reasoning powers, and trust Him to work through them, even when He may appear to act in contradiction to common sense.

To love the Lord my God with *all* my strength will involve a physical cost. I must give Him my body to indwell, and through which to speak, whether He chooses health or sickness, by strength or weakness, and trust Him utterly with the outcome.[8]

A treasure worth everything

Do we want to be like Jesus if it means such surrender of self? This is ultimately a question of desire. Jesus understood the power of desire in the choices we make and told two parables which touch on desire and also reveal His understanding of the cost and gain of sacrifice:

The kingdom of heaven is like treasure hidden in a field, which a man found and covered up. Then in his joy he goes and sells all that he has and buys that field. Again, the kingdom of heaven is like a merchant in search of fine pearls, who, on finding one pearl of great value, went and sold all that he had and bought it (Matt. 13:44–46).

In both parables, a man finds something of great value. The man in the first parable finds it unexpectedly. The merchant in the second parable has been looking for something like this all his life. In both parables, it costs everything to gain the treasure. What is striking in the first parable is the way the man went about giving up everything. "In his joy," Jesus says, "he goes and sells all that he has." It was as if Jesus wanted us to pay as much attention to his attitude as his actions. And so we pay attention. We think about what it means to have joy in our hearts and wonder how someone could have such joy in a situation like this? Yes, the treasure was of great worth, but this man would lose everything he had and get only one thing in return. How could he be glad when it would cost him so much?

Jesus emphasizes the attitude because it shows us what is in the man's heart and what we see there reveals how much he values the newly discovered treasure. The man has joy as he sells everything he has, because he values what he will gain more than what he will lose. It is very likely that the man already possesses some treasures. They may be of little value in the world's eyes but they are things which he values. Good things, such as a house and the furniture in it, and perhaps some animals which help put food on the table. Perhaps there are tools of his trade, if he is a tailor or carpenter or blacksmith. There may even be family heirlooms which have meaning and value, if not in the world's eyes at least to him. These are good things and desirable things, but they are now lesser things. He has found a greater treasure and everything else pales in comparison.

Jesus knows very well what He asks of us by stating that He is to be our Greatest Yes. He knows that when we give Him our complete loyalty, complete obedience and complete surrender, we stand to lose some things, perhaps many things. We might lose relationships which are important to us. We might lose popularity. In countries where Christians are persecuted, we might lose freedom and even our lives. We might have to give up desires which are natural but nonetheless harmful to a God-designed life if we indulge them. But Jesus asks us to pay such a cost because He knows that the one thing we gain is worth everything we may lose.

Taking up the cross and denying self are negative-sounding conditions, but they are followed by the one great positive of following Jesus. When Jesus becomes our Greater Yes, we gain the kingdom of God, and we are on our way to the life we are meant to live. We are on our way to becoming the real you and the real me. Real change comes with a cost but it also comes with gain. The cost is giving up everything we are apart from Christ in order to gain the greatest treasure we will ever have—Christ in us, the hope of glory.

The heart which has Jesus as its Greater Yes allows nothing to come between it and the One it loves:

> You have learnt the death of self when there is nothing between your bare heart and Jesus. . . . Christ is the beginning, and the end is Christ. The soul's first step is to let Him in as its life: the last step in a sense can go no further. It is only that the apprehension of Him has increased, and the hindrances and limitations have been swept away. Christ—Christ—Christ—filling all the horizon. Everything in us: everything to us: everything through us. To live is Christ.—Amen."[9]

REAL LIFE WITH A REAL GOD

"Every thought we hold, every decision we make, every action we take, every emotion we allow to shape our behaviour, every response we make to the world around us, every relationship we enter into, every reaction we have toward the things that surround us and impinge upon our lives—all of these things, little by little, are shaping us into some kind of being. We are being shaped into either the wholeness of the image of Christ or a horribly destructive caricature of that image—destructive not only to ourselves but also to others, for we inflict our brokenness upon them." –Robert Mulholland[10]

1. George was honest enough to admit, "I like Jesus, but I'm not so sure I want to be like Him." Time for honest reflection in God's presence:

   • What do I think about Jesus' terms of discipleship?
   • What will it mean in my life to follow Him so completely?

2. Real change begins with an honest question about desire. Do I really want to be like Christ? If the answer is yes, then it continues with a question of the will. Am I willing to do whatever it takes in order to become an image-bearer once again? Am I even willing to die to self?

3. Write down the conditions of being with Jesus that you find in the following passages. Talk with God about each one and what it will mean to apply them in your situation. Ask Him to reveal where you need to grow as a Christ-follower.

   Luke 9:23–24   Luke 14:25–35

4. Read Philippians 3:7–14. What challenges and encouragement do you see in these verses? Use this passage as a conversation with God. What is He saying to you and what do you want to say in response?

10

Two Red Dots

Dear Sir:
Regarding your article "What's Wrong with the World?" I am.
Yours truly.–G. K. Chesterton[1]

And I am sure of this, that he who began a good work in youwill
bring it to completion at the day of Jesus Christ. (Phil. 1:6)

The first six years of our ministry in Chad were spent in a rural town on the border of Sudan where we did our shopping in an open market which spread rather haphazardly along one side of a lake. One could see the entire market from the top of a small hill and, in one glance, I could determine exactly where I needed to go for the items on my list. After wandering in the afternoon sun through a labyrinth of market stalls and bargaining from stall to stall for the usual onions, potatoes and rice, I would often long for the convenience of a shopping center. Actually, I wanted more than a shopping center. I wanted a mega-mall. I wanted variety and lots of it, with air conditioning, and all in one place.

Our family is a long way from Chad these days. Our three children live in the United States with their spouses and children. Louis and I live in Singapore. Both countries are full of shopping centers and more than one qualifies as a mega-mall. The largest in Singapore is Vivo City which, happily, is only one metro stop away from our apartment. Such close proximity to nearly everything I could want or need is a luxury indeed, so I tend to do most of my shopping there.

Besides the luxury of convenience which shopping in Singapore allows, there is another difference from our Chadian shopping experience. We have lived in Singapore for two years, and although I have often shopped at Vivo City, I am still learning my way around this enormous mall. There are times when I wander through its vast labyrinth of stores, riding escalator after escalator, turning corner after corner, and long for the convenience of a small market space by a lake where I can see in one glance where I want to be.

Thankfully, on every level and in several corners of this mini-world of its own, there is a map. Locating one of these maps is itself a challenge, but I am beginning to know where they are. Once I stand in front of a map, I look for two locations. First, I locate where I want to be. After locating my destination of choice, I then look for where I am at that moment. This second location is usually marked conveniently on the map by a red dot which says "You are here." More often than not I discover that I am some distance from where I want to be. So I lift my head to look again at the bigger picture and trace the path I need to take to reach my destination.

I need two reference points on a map to make the physical journey through a mega-mall. I need to know where I want to be as well as where I currently am. The same is true for our spiritual journey. The bigger picture of life is designer living and how we are meant to live as image-bearers who respond to life and relate to those around us from our deepest place of significance and security. On this map of spiritual formation, there are the same two locations—where we want to be and where we currently are. We need both references if we are to grow as image-bearers. Unlike the map in the mall where there is only one red dot marked "You are here," our life with Christ has two red dots, and both are marked with the words "You are here."

As Christians, we live in two realities at the same time. One is the "You are here" red dot of what Christ has made possible through His sacrificial death and resurrection life. We are a new creation. The old life has gone, the new life has come. This is a present reality, not merely a hopeful future waiting for us in heaven. Today and every day, we can say "I am here"—fully redeemed, fully forgiven and with all the fullness of God available to me in Christ. The second reality is the "You are here" red dot of being a soul in process. Yes, we are a new creation, but in the words of Martin Luther, "all does not yet gleam in glory."[2] Today and every day, we also say "I am here"—with self-focus and its clinging cousins still lurking in the well of my soul.

I am here—a new creation

The writers of the New Testament state clearly that because of what Christ has accomplished on the cross and because of the work of the Holy Spirit in every believer's life, we are no longer where we used to be. This is a good thing when we realize who and what we were before the cross.

> And you were dead in the trespasses and sins . . . you were at that time separated from Christ, alienated from the commonwealth of Israel and strangers to the covenants of promise, having no hope and without God in the world.

You who once were far off have been brought near by the blood of Christ." (Eph.2:1, 12-13)

From death to life, from separation to union, from being excluded to included, from foreign to familiar, once far away and now brought near: "Therefore, if anyone is in Christ, he is a new creation. The old has passed away; behold, the new has come" (2 Cor. 5:17).

What kind of "new" are we? We are "holy and blameless and above reproach before him," Paul writes to the church, at Colossae (Col. 1:22). We possess "every spiritual blessing," he tells the church in Ephesus (Eph. 1:3). We have "all things that pertain to life and godliness," Peter informs Christ-followers who are living in the part of the world which is now modern-day Turkey (2 Pet. 1:3). Each statement is an "I am here" location for every person who has new life in Christ. No Christian can say to God, "The reason I still sin, the reason I am not changing, is because You have not given me what I need to make it possible."[3]

These are liberating truths which bring great hope and lead to real change. God Himself is at work in us "to will and to work for his good pleasure" (Phil. 2:13). Included in "everything we need" is the presence of Christ living in us and through us. Kenneth Boa reminds us, "This is the goal of the Christian life—a growing understanding of our union with Christ both in our thinking and in our practice."

As writers of the New Testament affirm, we can with full integrity, as persons redeemed by Christ's work on the cross and as new creations through the work of the Holy Spirit, say "I am here. Forgiven and redeemed. Holy in God's sight. Without blemish. Free from accusation. Able to live as an image-bearer once again. Christ has made it possible." This is a red dot reality for every person who is new in Christ. It is what we are to believe about God and about ourselves. The redemptive and restoring work of the cross is His final answer for our God-designed souls. We are not to return to the garden and doubt once again that what God has said about us is true.

When we take God at His Word and live in the "I am here" of a new creation in Christ, there are two results. The first is we begin to live with genuine humility. No one who realizes what lies in the depths of his soul and at the same time understands what Christ has done for him on the cross can bear a prideful heart. We will want to fall on our knees before God in humble gratitude. We do not naturally deserve nor have we done anything to earn this justification in His eyes, but we have it. Because it flows from a love and faithfulness which are intrinsic to God and not dependent on anything outside of Him, a love and faithfulness which are greater than any love or faithfulness we can give in return, we will never lose it. So we walk in humility and gratitude before God and the world.

The second result of taking God at His Word is to live with genuine hope. We are all too aware, at least I am, that no matter how sincerely we desire to "to walk in a manner worthy of the Lord, fully pleasing to him," as Paul writes to the Colossians (1:10), we miss the mark every day. Christ lives in us, yes, but so does the self and its clinging cousins. As much as we would like to put into practice the "No longer I" of an image-bearing life, there is still a great deal of "I" and not enough of Christ in the well of the soul, so to speak. This can be discouraging unless we believe God means what He says about our restoration.

Paul writes to the Philippian Christians that "he who began a good work in you will bring it to completion at the day of Jesus Christ" (Phil. 1:6). We do well to memorize this promise and remind ourselves of it every day when we feel our weakness and see so clearly our imperfections. God knows very well that we are not yet what we should be, but He is also doing something about it.

Humility and hope are the marks of a Christian. We are humbled by a grace which we never deserved and a status before God which we never earned. We are hopeful of real change because we are not alone in the process. And, yes, restoration as image-bearers is a process. This brings us to the second red dot reality of our life in Christ. This other "You are here" is equally true and equally affirmed by New Testament writers.

I am here—a soul in process

Although Christ lives in me now, there is also much of the old self still in residence and it greatly influences the way I live. I am still impatient, prone to criticism and sensitive to criticism from others. As much as I long to reflect Christ in the way I live, I can still be uncaring, unforgiving, truth-bending and image-protecting . . . the list goes on. Christ in me is a reality, but growth in Christ-life is a process.

Jesus likened salvation from sin to a new birth. Like all babies, when we are spiritually new-born, we know nothing about how to live. We must learn, and learning of any kind is done best when we engage in the process. At the same time that our transformation "comes from the Lord who is the Spirit" (2 Cor. 3:18), we have our own part in the Spirit's transforming work. God works in us "to will and to work for his good pleasure" (Phil. 2:13), but we are to cooperate with him by intentional willing and working. We are told to "grow in the grace and knowledge of our Lord and Savior Jesus Christ" (2 Pet. 3:18). We are to "put off the old self" and "put on the new self" (Eph. 4:22, 24). We are to "put to death" God-dishonoring attitudes which lead to God-dishonoring actions and "put on" Christ-like attitudes which lead to Christ-like actions (Col. 3:5, 10). We are to "train" ourselves to be godly (1 Tim. 4:7). All are words which evoke images of intentional and disciplined effort.

I must admit that although I fully understand growth is a process which requires time, I have often wished that God would speed it up. Because He is so powerful, I believe He could if He wanted to. Yet in His infinitely greater wisdom than mine, He has, in the words of Fénelon, "willed that men should grow up through the weakness and troubles of childhood, instead of being born fully developed men"[4] and has also willed that Christians should grow into the likeness of Christ through a similar process, weakness and troubles included.

What particular path God chooses for getting me from one red dot to the other and however long it will take to make this journey is up to Him. But how I respond to the weaknesses I feel and troubles I experience along the way is up to me. In fact, becoming aware of how I respond is part of the spiritual formation process. There are three unhealthy ways that I can respond to how often I miss the mark in reflecting Christ. They are discouragement, frustration and blame. Each of these is a natural response but is also tied to the self-life that lurks within and if allowed to go unchecked can hinder change.

Discouragement

Discouragement is a response to our weaknesses that can, if we are not careful, lead to an unhealthy lowering of expectations, both of myself and of God. This was what Glenn was tempted to do as we talked together in the coffee shop. Discouragement is a natural emotion, and we all feel discouraged from time to time. Not every sense of discouragement is evidence of failure or lack of trust in God, and it is important to remember this, or we will become discouraged that we get discouraged. Prolonged discouragement, however, becomes unhealthy to the soul. An unhealthy focus on weakness and imperfection can lead us to think that it's just not possible to live by God's standards and consequently, we stop trying.

Awareness that we cannot live by God's standards is, on one level, a sign of humility. There is truth in this, as God reminded me long ago and as I reminded Glenn. In particular, the kind of love that we see in Jesus and are told to show each other is not natural to us. It is a God-love and only God can give it to us. Neither can we attain to God's holiness or wholeness of life on our own. Brokenness is in our nature and only God's presence and fullness can make us whole again.

Acceptance of brokenness keeps us humble, but brokenness is only half of the gospel message. If we use brokenness as a reason for not changing in character and losing hope, we leave behind the truth of God's indwelling presence and His transforming work through the Spirit. If we allow brokenness to discourage us to the point of giving up on holiness and wholeness, we are in fact saying that God has saved us but can't do anything more.

Fénelon goes so far as to suggest that "discouragement is simply the despair of wounded self-love."[5] In other words, pride can be at the root of discouragement. We want to be perfect and it bothers us that we aren't. It especially bothers us when our imperfection and weakness is evident to others. "The real way of profiting by the humiliation of one's faults," Fénelon advises, "is to face them in their true hideousness, without ceasing to hope in God."[6]

Facing our faults without ceasing to hope in God is key to restoration. Honesty admits that we are imperfect people who often get it wrong rather than perfect people who always get it right. Hope declares that God is doing something about us. My personal definition of a church is that we are a community of sinners saved by grace helping each other become all God means us to be. Broken, yes, but being made whole again. Patient in the process, relying on grace from God and each other, declaring truth in loving ways and growing in the likeness of Christ. A community of Christ-followers should be one of the safest places for us to be honest about who we are without being overly discouraged in the process.

Discouragement is a natural emotional response to life (one only needs to read through the Psalms to see this is true), but it can be a healthy or unhealthy discouragement depending on what we do with it. A healthy discouragement leads to honesty and humility and a renewed focus on God for the help and strength we need. Unhealthy discouragement, on the other hand, leads us from God-focus to self-focus and eventually keeps us from growing.

Frustration

A second response to weakness and imperfection is frustration. Frustration, like discouragement, is a natural emotional response that becomes unhealthy if allowed to remain in the well of the soul. Frustration can also resemble a humble God-focus but can have self-focus at the root. Andrew Murray writes in *The Master's Indwelling*, "What is it that often disturbs our hearts, and our peace? It is pride seeking to be something."[7]

We usually associate "pride seeking to be something" with secular pursuits. Seeking success, fame, youth, beauty or status. Seeking to be something or someone important. But Andrew Murray is writing about spiritual pursuits, not secular. It is possible to be frustrated in what are desirable spiritual pursuits—a level of maturity we want, effectiveness in ministry, respect and esteem as a spiritual leader. These are good pursuits, but being frustrated when we don't attain them is evidence that there is more "I" in me than Christ. Once again, Fénelon writes with penetrating insight in *The Royal Way of the Cross*: "It is the 'I' which makes you so keen and sensitive. You want God as well as man to be always satisfied with you, and you want to be satisfied with yourself in all your dealings with God."[8]

Fénelon counseled and mentored a wide range of people in the seventeenth century church. Those who knew him or received counsel through his personal and public letters gained a deeper understanding of the soul in process, and his letters contain much wisdom for us today. Whenever I read Fénelon, he compels me to be ruthlessly honest in my oh-so-quick claims to live for Christ alone:

> Almost all who aim at serving God do more or less for their own sake. They want to win, not to lose: to be comforted, not to suffer; to possess, not to be deprived; to increase, not to diminish. It is self-love which makes us so inconsolable at seeing our imperfections. Self-love

cannot bear to see itself. . . . The greater our own self-love the more severe critics we shall be. . . . God does not like souls which are self-absorbed, and are always, so to speak, looking at themselves in a mirror.[11]

Ouch. Yes, if the truth be told, I would rather win than lose. I prefer comfort over suffering. There are times when I would like people to consider me a spiritual person not only for Christ's sake, but . . . well . . . for my own. When it comes to diminishing vs. increasing, if we're talking about body size, I'm all for it, but Fénelon is referring to deeper things. He means a willingness to decrease in the eyes of the world and a willingness to be "small" and unnoticed. He means the ability to let someone else have attention or affirmation or success without needing it for myself. The words of John the Baptist in referring to Jesus, "He must increase, but I must decrease" (John 3:30) always come to mind as I read Fénelon.

Thankfully, Fénelon does not leave us with awareness of self-life without counseling what to do about it. He writes to a friend from his own experience, "I know what it is to be weak; I am a thousand times weaker than you. It is very profitable to have realized what one is; but do not add to that weakness, which is inseparable from our human nature, an estrangement from the very means of strength."[12]

We are to bring our weakness and imperfection to God, not let them keep us from Him. "To see ourselves perfectly, self-love must be rooted up, and the love of God reign solely in us. Then the same light which shows our faults would remove them. Till then we only half know ourselves, because we are only half-given to God, cleaving to self a great deal more than we think or dare to admit to ourselves." Fénelon adds, with what I imagine must have been a twinkle in his eye: "Self-love speaks less when it sees that we pay no attention to it."[11]

Frustration is a natural response when things aren't going the way we would like, but it can also be a form of self-love paying attention to itself. It can be a red-dot "Here I am" self-focus even in a desirable pursuit of holiness. Frustration, like discouragement, becomes unhealthy when it keeps our focus on self rather than on God. Both discouragement and frustration resemble humility but only in part. True humility, in the words of Fénelon, "lies in seeing our own unworthiness and giving ourselves up to God, never doubting that he can work out the greatest results in us and for us."[12]

Blame

The third unhealthy response to missing the mark in our attempts to live as we are meant to live is to blame others for our inability to do so. This response can also sound like a pursuit of godliness but has a noticeable whine in the voice:

> "I am trying to be loving, but my coworker is so critical of me all the time."

> "I am trying to be more patient but my teenager keeps pushing my button."

> "I am trying to keep my thoughts pure, but the women in my office dress so immodestly."

> "I want to be honest but she will be hard to live with if I tell her the truth."

It also sounds suspiciously like Adam and Eve when they excused themselves from personal responsibility in the Handover:

Adam to God: "Eve is the one who offered me the fruit (the woman you gave me, by the way). She's the one you should focus on here, not me." (see Gen. 3:12)

Eve to both Adam and God: "No, that's not fully true. I wouldn't have eaten it at all if the serpent hadn't been so deceptive. And (with a pointed look in God's direction) what was he doing in the garden, anyway?" (see Gen. 3:13)

Blame is a hammer which we all wield from time to time, but it is an especially useful tool for image-projectors. The hammer of blame has two cousins in the "Self Clan" written on each side of its handle: self-defense and self-deception. Self-defense murmurs in the ear, "No doubt you have some issues to work on, too, but she makes it difficult for you to be patient." Self-deception uses another tactic: "You are not the problem. If he would be less sensitive to everything you say, you could get along better. When he changes, things will improve."

Blaming someone else is never a healthy response to the challenges we face in living a Christ-like life. It may well be true that the other person needs to change, but I am responsible before God for my way of relating and responding, not for his. I cannot wait for someone else to change before I choose to love as Christ calls me to love. My thoughts, actions, reactions and choices are to be shaped by the Christ who lives in me, not by the people around me. Neither can I see the log in my own eye while I focus on the speck in others.

The Serenity Prayer is well-known and oft-quoted in the Christian world. There are a few altered versions of this prayer, some of which are more humorous than serious. My prayer for the last few years is one of the humorous versions, but I pray it seriously: "Lord, grant me the serenity to accept the one I cannot change, the courage to change the one I can, and the wisdom to know it's me."

"It is the I in you and me that blinds the eyes," writes Amy Carmichael. "The loss of I, that I may know Him, see Him with new clearness in all creation…May the Lord grant this to us all."[13]

Discouragement, frustration, blame. I am prone to them all. Each one is a possible red dot reality on the big picture of a soul in process. "I am here, Lord, discouraged that I haven't changed more by now." "I am here, Lord, so frustrated that I keep interrupting people when I want to be a better listener." "I am here, Lord, too quick to blame others for my attitudes."

A growing awareness of how easily I respond in unhealthy ways and of the pride at the root of my responses can also be discouraging until I turn my eyes away from the mirror of self and once again see "no longer I but Christ." When I remind myself of Amy Carmichael's words that "from Him there is never a rebuke for human weakness"[14] and when I take God at His Word and remember the twin truths of redemption and restoration, I can respond to weakness and imperfection with a more healthy response, which is to be honest with God and remain hopeful of His help.

Honesty

Honesty does not come easily, but honesty is essential to transformation. Scripture tells us that the one who may dwell with God is not only "He who walks blamelessly and does what is right" but who "speaks truth in his heart" (Ps.

15:2). The psalmist also declares of God: "Behold, you delight in truth in the inward being, and you teach me wisdom in the secret heart" (Ps. 51:6).

Most of us are honest to a certain degree, but many are not willing to go to the depth of honesty which is needed for real change. This can be too painful. I for one find it painful to see evidence of selfishness, pride, anger, fear or any of the self-life that God reveals is lurking within, but I will not reach where I sincerely want to be in life with Christ until I am honest about where I am. Finding and naming the red dot of my current spiritual state is a necessary step toward changing it.

A surface honesty is easy enough to attain. Admitting brokenness and imperfection in a general way is not painful, because, after all, aren't we all imperfect? I can even easily admit that I am not gifted or competent in some domains. For instance, I would love to sing like Celine Dion but I can't. Honesty on this point is not difficult since my vocal limitations are all too obvious when I belt out a song at the top of my voice. I can also admit that I am not the one you would automatically turn to for practical help in a crisis. My physician husband has the calmness and quickness of thought needed to respond in ways that would actually be of help. You would do better just to ask me to pray.

Such levels of honesty are not a threat to the ego and don't seriously damage one's image, but to reveal that we are easily irritated, often defensive or have a critical spirit that rises up more than we wish it would . . . these admissions do not come so easily. Such depths of honesty might cause people to question our spirituality. It might make the members of our community think less of us if we admit that we have a problem.

Surface admissions are safe, but deeper admissions bring judgment and misunderstanding, two things which image-projection wants to avoid. On the other hand, it's very possible that such admissions will surprise no one. Others often see in us what we cannot see or don't want to see in ourselves.

Real change

Real change happens when I bring the real me, a soul in process, to the real God; when I name my spiritual location of the moment: "I am here, God," filled with self and its clinging cousins. It helps to remember that God already sees the depths of the heart and mind, for "the LORD searches all hearts and understands every plan and thought" (1 Chron. 28:9). We bring nothing new to God's attention with the honest admissions of a red dot of the moment.

It also helps to remember His forgiveness and grace. "The soul of the wounded cries for help; yet God charges no one with wrong" (Job 24:12). A healthy response admits my imperfections and weaknesses while resting in God's grace and trusting in His transforming power.

Honesty moves me from self-reliance to a humble and hopeful God-reliance. Honesty, humility, God-reliance and trust reverse the choices made at the Great Handover of the soul. When I move from self-reliance to God-reliance, I reverse Eve's choice to live apart from God. When I believe the truth of Christ-in-me, I reverse Eve's decision to believe the enemy of her soul rather than the lover of her soul. God's Word becomes my final answer. Finally, my honest conversation with God about where I fail to live well for Him is a reversal of Adam's and Eve's conversation with God after they disobeyed.

When we return to the account of the Great Handover to see what happened after Eve and Adam ate the fruit, we learn that they are hiding. God calls to Adam, "Where are you?" and when Adam comes out of hiding, they begin a conversation which is marked, as we have already noted, on Adam's side by deception and blame rather than honesty. What might have happened if Adam had said, "Here I am, God, disobedient and self-serving, unfaithful to You and distrusting. I know I was wrong and I need your mercy. I hope You'll forgive me and help me to make it right." We will never know what would have happened, because this is not what Adam said. In fact, Adam and Eve rejected God twice on this fateful day. The first rejection was when they listened to the words of His enemy over believing and obeying His Word. The second was when they hid themselves from Him rather than trusting Him for forgiveness and restoration.

Despite what Adam and Eve said to God, He was well aware of the true state of things and responded in three ways. Firstly, He allowed the consequences of their disobedience. Sin entered the created world and left its mark. Spiritual death and separation from God became the new reality.

Secondly, He immediately set in place the process that would lead to restoration. Even as God pronounced to Adam and Eve the consequences of sin in their personal lives as well as the world, He gave a promise of deliverance. One day Satan would be defeated and the crushing would come through the offspring of a woman (see Gen. 3:15).

Thirdly, God cared for Adam and Eve in their brokenness. In what can only be seen as a poignant and deeply personal act of grace, "The LORD God made for Adam and for his wife garments of skins and clothed them" (see Gen.

3:21). Adam and Eve had betrayed God and handed over their souls to Satan, yet with His own hands, He fashioned better clothes for them than the makeshift fig leaves they had hastily donned in their newly awakened awareness of self. Truth and grace were at work from the beginning.

Two spiritual realities

Two red dots keep us honest, keep us humble and give us hope. Two spiritual realities declare "I am here"—a new creation with all that I need for image-bearing- and "I am here"—self-serving, self-focused, self-righteous. All does not yet gleam in glory, but all is being purified.

Jack Miller, founder of World Harvest Mission, often declared two "cheer ups" for the Christian life. The first keeps us humble and the second gives us hope.

"*Cheer up! You're worse than you think you are.*" I find this truth incredibly freeing. To admit "Here I am, God, and it's worse than I thought" means no more pretense before God and before others. It means no more image-projecting. There is rest in laying down the effort to be what I cannot be in my own strength. There is also rest in the second declaration which comes fast on the heels of the first: "*Cheer up! God's grace is greater than you could ever imagine.*"

Awareness of sin is balanced by awareness of grace. "Between here and heaven, every minute that the Christian lives will be a minute of grace," writes Charles Spurgeon.[15] God's grace met my hopeless condition at the cross and did something about it. He gave me new life and through Christ restored His image to my soul. God, in His grace, sees my weakness as an image-bearer and, through the transforming work of the Spirit, is doing something about it.

REAL LIFE WITH A REAL GOD

"Make use of your imperfections to learn detachment from yourself and cleave to God only." –François Fénelon[16]

1. Honesty: Read Gen. 3:8–13, the account of Adam and Eve's conversation with God after their disobedience. Where is honesty missing in this conversation? Where is honesty missing in my own conversations with God? How will honesty with God make a difference in my hope of change?

2. Humility: Eph. 2 gives a "before and after" picture of spiritual life. Read through the chapter noting who you were before life with Christ and who you are now.

3. Hope: As you read the verses, reflect on the following questions: What is a "done deal" in my life because of Christ? What is possible for me because of the Holy Spirit?

   John 3:3–8   2 Cor. 3:18; 5:17
   Rom. 6:1–7, 14   Col. 1:22

4. Naming the red dot: Ask the Holy Spirit to make you aware of the self-life at work in your daily life. Think of ordinary situations in which the way you respond may be an indication of an area needing soul work.

   a. Have you tried on clothing in the glaring light of a dressing room and are feeling depressed after seeing yourself physically in the mirror? Talk with God about your red dot of discouragement and self-pity: "Here I am, God, feeling sorry for myself. I know You love me as I am, but I still wish I had a better figure. Help me live from my place of deepest significance and not from what I see in the mirror."

b. Are you aware of irritation toward a coworker and keep wishing he would change to make things easier for you? Talk with God about your red dot of a critical spirit and tendency to overlook the log in your own eye: "Here I am, God, thinking he's the problem and not me. Help me see him with Your eyes. Help me grow in Christ-like ways of relating to others."

11

Practices that Transform

Instead of asking the Lord to change our circumstances to suit us, we can ask Him to use our circumstances to change us.–Kenneth Boa[1]

The spirit of man is the lamp of the LORD, searching all his innermost parts.(Prov. 20:27)

Someone has said that holiness consists not in heroic acts but in a thousand small decisions. I agree and would also add that growth in holiness is forged not in the big events of life but in a thousand smaller events. Every day we participate in the process of restoration through decisions and responses which move us either toward restoration as image-bearers or away from it. Robert Mulholland reminds us that:

> Every thought we hold, every decision we make, every action we take, every emotion we allow to shape our behavior, every response we make to the world around us, every relationship we enter into, every reaction we have toward the things that surround us and impinge upon our lives—all of these things, little by little, are shaping us into some kind of being. We are being shaped into either the wholeness of the image of Christ or a horribly destructive caricature of that image—destructive not only to ourselves but also to others, for we inflict our brokenness on them.[2]

Thankfully, we have seen that we are not alone in this process. God is at work to fulfill His purpose of restoration (see Phil. 2:13) through the Holy Spirit who is at work transforming us into the likeness of Christ (see 2 Cor. 3:18) and coming alongside us as helper and enabler (see John 14:17, 26; see Rom. 8:2, 5). These truths are encouraging, to say the least. I really do not want to inflict my brokenness on the people around me, but I do so on a daily basis as I react and respond from the self-life which still lurks within. I need divine help if such desperately needed real and deep change is going to happen.

Ruth Haley Barton in her excellent book, *Strengthening the Soul of Your Leadership*, agrees that change is something we cannot produce on our own:

> In the process of transformation the Spirit of God moves us from behaviors motivated by fear and self-protection to trust and abandonment to God; from selfishness and self-absorption to freely offering the gifts of my authentic self; from the ego's desperate attempts to control the outcomes of our lives to an ability to give ourselves over to the will of God which is often the foolishness of the world. This kind of change is not something we can produce or manufacture for ourselves but it is what we most need. It is what those around us need.[3]

Without the Spirit's help, my part in restoration of the soul can become little more than an exercise in self-analysis. With the Spirit's help, it becomes, in the words of J.I. Packer, a "self-search in God's presence."[4] Without the Spirit's help, I am prone to deception, since I have a tendency to be easily satisfied with myself and think I'm doing well enough as long as external behavior is acceptable. The Spirit of truth, however, will not let me get away with surface spirituality. Anything that keeps me from reflecting God's glory in the world and from living as He has designed me to live needs to die.

In *Rediscovering Holiness*, J.I. Packer notes that although "some sins are intrinsically greater and intrinsically worse than others, there can be no small sins against a great God."[5] Through the spotlight of the Holy Spirit,

> "God searches our hearts as well as weighing our actions," exposing the self-life in "our motives and our purposes, as well as in our performance. . . . In one sense, indeed, it is true to say that God focuses more attention on the heart—the thinking, reacting, desiring, decision-making core and center of our being—than He does on the deeds done, for it is by what goes on in the our hearts that we are most truly known to Him."[6]

So when I say with the psalmist, "Search me, O God, and know my heart! Try me and know my thoughts! And see if there be any grievous way in me, lead me in the way everlasting!" (Ps. 139:23–24), God takes me at my word and shines the Holy Spirit's searchlight on the areas of self-life that are still alive and active in my soul. My part is to pay attention to what the Spirit reveals and to cooperate with God for change.

Paying attention in our relationships

With a sincere desire to know what needs to die so that my true self being renewed in Christ can live, I begin a practice of paying attention. I pay attention to the feelings and thoughts that rise up from within as I interact with the people around me and as I respond to the situations that come my way each day. The practice of paying attention is not an easy one. I am always challenged and humbled by what the Spirit reveals. Any day of the week could resemble the following:

It's 6:00 a.m. and I am spending time with God to begin the day. Alone with God, immersed in conversation with Him and reading His Word, I am at peace with the world. Love for Christ rises up within as I read through another chapter in the Gospel of Luke and see Him in action. I see how He looks at people with compassion and hear how He speaks with life-giving words. I long to be the same way and so I ask God to help me be life-giving in the coming day, and I sincerely mean it.

This is the real me. Loving Christ and wanting to be like Him in the way I live.

It's now 8:00 a.m. and I am walking to the office. On the way, I see a neighbor whose attitude has a tendency to challenge my peace. The minute I see him, I sense that he is in a usual grumpy mood and wish he would wipe the sour expression off his face once in a while. In a flash, a critical spirit fills the space that was ready to love the world just a few minutes before. "Do not let your peace depend on what people say of you" wrote Thomas à Kempis,[7] and I would add "nor let it be in the looks of men," but my peace is often affected by my neighbor's sour look and critical comments, and my response to him more often than not is irritation. Not wanting the subject of my irritation to suspect anything, I arrange my face into a smile and greet him as I pass by.

This is also the real me. Irritated and ungracious on the inside while smiling and greeting on the outside. I don't want to be this way, but there it is: irritation and image-projection rising up spontaneously from within. The old proverb is true, "What's in the well comes out."

Two red dots are located, and it's only the beginning of my day. "Here I am" loving Christ and desiring to honor Him in the well of my soul. "Here I am" responding to a neighbor with an irritation that rises up whenever we meet. Rubbing shoulders with humanity has a way of producing irritation rather than worship and pettiness rather than praise.

We do well to pay attention in our relationships. Robert Mulholland suggests that we see in every relationship a potential place for a transforming encounter with God:

> The place where we live out our relationship of loving union with God is not in the quiet of our prayer closet but in our relationships with one another. . . . We can't be compassionate in the quiet of our prayer closet but only in the often difficult and unpleasant noise of our relationship with another person. We can't be kind all by ourselves but only in a relationship, and particularly when we are tempted to be unkind or mean rather than to be kind. We can't be lowly in the privacy of our room but only in relationships with others, and especially in those relationships where our impulse is to exalt ourselves over others. We can't be humble with ourselves but only in our life with others, particularly where our pride tends to surface. We can't be patient by ourselves but only in relationships with others and predominantly in those where impatience is the norm.[8]

I have learned to thank God for the people in my life who challenge my patience or disturb my peace. Without them, I would not see how impatient I can be and how little love I really have. Through them, I become aware of self-focus, self-service, self-protection, self-defense, even self-righteousness, in the ways that I think and relate. I am sorry to see these things in my soul, but by God's grace, He is changing me and in each challenging relationship I have an opportunity to see where I still need to grow.

Paying attention in our circumstances

The Spirit also uses our circumstances to reveal what is not Christlike in the well of the soul. We should especially pay attention to the ordinary circumstances which happen in the course of a day and may seem too commonplace or familiar to be significant. It is in the ordinary, commonplace rubs of life and how we respond to them that we also see what lies within.

What do we feel when an idea we have proposed at work or in a group is rejected? Does a twinge of resentment or discouragement well up? Do we focus on the rejection rather than what we can learn from it? Do we make it personal when it was really an objective decision, having nothing to do with us? This may mean pride needs to be addressed or that self-defense or self-pity is in the well of the soul. What about when a friend cancels a lunch date? Do we take it personally and begin to think it says something about how the friend feels about us? This indicates that self-referenced thinking is at work, meaning we tend to relate everything that happens to us personally. A twinge of jealousy when someone else is complimented suggests self-promotion is in the soul. Walking past a store and feeling an urge to go in and buy something, even though we don't need another new thing, suggests inner compulsions at work which need to be addressed.

Each of these situations is an ordinary circumstance which can occur many moments in a day and we are hardly aware of how we respond, but the Spirit uses them to shed light on where we need to grow spiritually if we pay attention.

Paying attention in our conversations

Another arena where the Spirit sheds light, if I am paying attention, is in the conversations I have during the day. Paying attention to what happens inside of me while listening in a conversation can help me identify areas of self-life which need to be dealt with in order for Christ-life to grow.

It is possible to listen to someone and at the same time be aware of what I am feeling and thinking. What am I feeling as I talk with this person? Am I feeling defensive? Guarded? Am I secretly mocking even as I am outwardly nodding approval? Am I feeling a need to be witty or a need to add something spiritual or profound to the conversation? Am I really listening or am I merely waiting for a chance to say what I want to say? When I become aware of what is happening inside of me as I talk with others, I can name the "I am here" of self and its clinging cousins. I can admit an attitude which does not honor Christ and harms the people I relate to, and I can bring it to God for transformation.

Paying attention to what I am thinking or feeling when listening to the words of others is one way to see where I need to change, but paying attention to my own words when in conversations can also be revealing. Jesus said that "out of the overflow of the heart the mouth speaks." Words, especially those spoken in unguarded moments, reveal what is in the heart.

Do I sometimes exaggerate or tell only part of a truth?

Do I speak negatively about others when they are not around?

Do I have a tendency to dominate conversations?

Do I jump to conclusions and finish someone else's sentence?

Do I move into teaching mode even in a social conversation?

It can be helpful to set aside time in God's presence to think about recent conversations we have had and recent circumstances we have faced. Pulling away from the madding crowd gives the physical and emotional space needed for honest reflection. Alone with God, we can ask questions similar to the questions in this chapter. We also ask God to keep us honest and the Holy Spirit to shed light on where we need to grow. In this way we engage in a "self-search in God's presence."

This "self-search in God's presence" is best when alone with God and free of distractions, but it can happen in the midst of a busy day as well. We do not need to wait until we are out of a situation, away from people or alone with God to bring our self-life to Him for transformation. In fact, some of the most transformational work of the Spirit can happen in the very moment we become aware of a prideful thought or self-serving motive. In that first moment of awareness, we can turn the exposed self-life over to God and enable transformation as self-focus returns to God-focus and self-life makes room for Christ-life. These "on the spot" moments of transformation can happen in the middle of a conversation or in the short space of a walk from one corner of the office to another. Because we live in the presence of God and walk with Him and talk with Him throughout the day, at any moment we can turn our thoughts into prayer, turn self-focus to God-focus and exchange self-life for Christ-life.

Prayers that transform

The goal of paying attention is spiritual growth and the goal of spiritual growth is to become like Christ. What we do with what the Spirit reveals should always move us towards Christ-life. Paying attention to what rises up within is only one part of the process. It helps to identify the "Here I am" of a sin-damaged self-life which needs to die. But I also need to embrace the "Here I am" of life in Christ.

- Here I am, Lord, full of pride and resentment. Get self-importance out of the way and fill me with Your humility.
- Here I am, Lord, letting my sense of self be determined by someone other than You. Trade my self-pity for the significance and security I have in You.
- Here I am, Lord, needing to be noticed in order to feel good about myself. Replace my self-serving with Your sacrificial servant heart.
- Here I am, Lord, never satisfied with what I have, always reaching for something else to make me happy. Trade my dissatisfaction for Your wholly satisfying life in me.

Amy Carmichael writes of a man who had a quick temper and was never in a place where he could go away to pray for help. "His habit was to send up a little telegraph prayer, 'Thy sweetness, Lord!' and sweetness came. Do you need courage? 'Thy courage, Lord!' Patience? 'Thy patience,

Lord!' Love? 'Thy love, Lord!' Shall we practice this swift
and simple way of prayer more and more? If we do, our Very
Present Help will not disappoint us. For Thou, Lord, hast
never failed them that seek Thee."[9]

Transformational prayers take less time than it takes
to text a friend, because God is nearer than we can ever
imagine. He is so near that a whisper of the heart can reach
him. A spontaneous prayer of repentance keeps us living in
grace. A prayer "on the spot" changes a critical thought into
a conversation with God. Prayers that "release and receive"
set in motion the divine exchange of Christ-life for self-life.
Each of these prayers can be done at any moment of the
day, whether we're walking through the door of a restaurant,
standing in line at the bank or sitting in a business meeting
listening to a report.

Prayers of repentance pave the way to real change. Leo
Tolstoy once commented that "everybody thinks of changing
the world, but nobody thinks of changing himself."[10] Transformational prayers focus on changing myself rather than
someone else, and true transformation always begins with
personal repentance. We have already seen that real desire
is essential for real change. Equally important is real repentance. We can be sorry for a dozen things in the course of a
day but not sorry enough to cooperate with the Holy Spirit
for change. In the same way, we can feel a sense of guilt for
personal actions and attitudes which we know are not hon-
oring to God, but not enough guilt to do something about
them. For example, I can feel a twinge of regret each time I
interrupt someone in a conversation. I can even wish I would
stop doing so, but twinges of regret and wishful thinking do
not equal repentance nor do they move me to change.

Repentance is a significant element of change in both the Old and New Testaments. The Old Testament use of repentance carries the idea of a change of direction. The Hebrew word for repentance is used to describe the shadow which God caused to move ten steps back on the stairway in 2 Kings 10:9–11. It is also used in reference to Israel's return from exile. In the Old Testament references, then, "to repent" means a reversal of direction or a return to one's point of departure. In the New Testament, to repent carries the sense of changing one's mind about something which causes one's actions to change as well. John the Baptist told the people coming to him for baptism to "Bear fruits in keeping with repentance" (Luke 3:8). In Paul's preaching, he called people to repent and turn to God but also to perform "deeds in keeping with their repentance" (Acts 26:20).

Prayers of personal repentance acknowledge that we need to change something more than behavior. We are not merely sorry for the things we have done and the ways that we think. True repentance includes sorrow that we are the kind of people who would do such things and think such ways. In many ways, a prayer of genuine repentance, one that understands the gospel and our need for grace, is less about what we have done and more about who we are without Christ.

Often the awareness of sin or self comes in a flash of awareness. Because it comes in the middle of a conversation or when we are engaged in work, there is no time to pull away to talk with God about what the Spirit has revealed. There is only time for one simple whisper of the soul to God: "Lord Jesus, have mercy on me, a sinner." This short and simple prayer is known in church history as the Jesus prayer and it is often all I have time for in the course of a day and with the numerous times I am aware of self, but it is all that is needed for the moment. There is neither pride nor deceit in the prayer of a humble and contrite heart, and short as it is, this prayer brings me immediately to the throne of mercy and grace.

It is enough for my heart to look up for a brief moment even if my eyes are focused on the person I am with. In that moment, I ask God's mercy and know that I receive it. In that moment, transformation has begun. Brief as it is, this prayer of repentance turns me away from focus on self to focus on God, and that in itself is the beginning of change.

Turning thoughts into prayer is a transformational practice which also helps us live more fully in awareness of God's presence. "Our life always expresses our dominant thoughts," notes Søren Kierkegaard. What we are thinking eventually shows in our faces and in our behavior, so it is a good idea to let God shape what we are thinking. And since we are constantly thinking, there is much we can say to God if we develop the habit of turning our thoughts into prayer.

This applies to all of our thoughts and not just the ones which reveal self-life. Joyful, thankful, surprised, or anxious thoughts . . . all can become a means of talking with God. I recently received a package from a friend and immediately thought, "She is so special." Out of habit, the thought became a conversation with God bringing Him into my joy of the moment. "Thank You for Becky. She is a gift to me and I'm sure You bless many people through her. Bless her today, God. Let her know Your presence and joy."

The same is true for unkind, resentful, prideful or lustful thoughts . . . these are opportunities to practice the presence of God in a different way. Instead of letting a God-dishonoring line of thinking go unchecked, we stop it at the moment of awareness and talk with God about it. "Lord, here I am again, jumping to conclusions. I'm sorry that I so quickly assume he's against me. Help me to change." "Lord, I'm feeling really insecure now, and I'm not sure why. Help me to rest in You and just do my best." "Lord, I really don't care about this. And I don't want to have this conversation. But I know You care and You want me to be here. Help me to care."

As God answers our prayer to "lead us in the way everlasting"(Ps. 139:24, NASB) and the Spirit reveals the "offensive ways in us," (139:14) we will have much to talk with Him about as we turn our self-dominated thoughts into prayer. Like prayers of repentance, these are short prayers, but they change us. The moment we turn an unkind thought into a conversation with God, we break its control over us. We put it somewhere other than our mind. Darkness cannot exist with light, and as we talk with God we are living in the light.

Prayers that renounce and receive name a specific sin and renounce its control over us but also establishes in its place an opposite redeeming character of Christ. For pride there is the humility of Christ. For lust there is His holiness. For deception there is His truth. For a tendency to manipulate and control, there is the filling of His Spirit. For self-centeredness there is His servant heart. For resentment and bitterness, there is His forgiveness. For a critical spirit there is His grace. For indifference there is His compassion. For rejection there is His unconditional love. These prayers can also be done at the moment we are aware of self at work.

"Father, I'm sorry for my critical spirit. I renounce its control on my life and receive in its place the humility of Christ."

"I'm sorry, Lord, that I'm feeling so jealous and want to be equally admired. I renounce self-promotion and self-pity, and receive the contentment of Christ."

"I repent of pride, Lord. I renounce its control on my life and receive the humility of Christ."

"I release self-pity and receive my identity in Christ as fully known and fully loved."

When there is no time to pray even these few words, a habit of turning to God at the moment of awareness can be as brief as a trusting prayer for His character to be in us, just as Amy Carmichael observed in the man she wrote about. "Your love, Lord," as we approach the difficult co-worker. "Your patience, Lord," as we feel impatience rising up within. "Your compassion, Lord" as we sense coldness in our hearts. "Your response, Lord" in place of our own.

Prayers of honesty are perhaps among the most transformational. God knows the depths of the heart and mind. According to the psalmist, "You know when I sit down and when I rise up; you discern my thoughts from afar... Even before a word is on my tongue, behold, O Lord, you know it altogether" (Ps. 139:2–4). With such a clear view of everything, I may as well acknowledge to God the red dot of sinful attitudes, self-serving motives and self-referenced ways of responding. He sees them long before I am aware of them.

It is indeed painful to see all that is not as it should be in my life, but honesty and hope keep me from self-pity and despair. God is intent on my restoration and uses the furnace of relationships and circumstances to burn away the dross and shape my soul. I for one am glad that He cares enough to make sure that restoration happens even if it means using the furnace of relationships and circumstances to do so.

In the Old Testament book of Malachi, God is likened to "a refiner and purifier of silver" (3:3). While reflecting on this verse, Amy Carmichael wrote of visiting a village goldsmith in the village in India where she lived:

"The picture of the Refiner is straight from Eastern life. The Eastern goldsmith sits on the floor by his crucible. For me, at least, it is not hard to know why the heavenly Refiner has to sit so long. The heart knows its own dross.

'How do you know how long to sit and wait? How do you know when it is purified?' we asked our village goldsmith.

'When I can see my face in it,' he replied.

Blessed be the love that never wearies, never gives up hope that, even in such poor metal our Father may at last see the reflection of His face."[11]

Real Life with a Real God

"Disciplines allow us to place ourselves before God so that He can transform us."– Richard Foster[12]

1. Read Isaiah 30:15. What is the relationship between repentance and rest? Between quietness and trust? How might these relate to becoming our true selves?

2. Read Psalm 139 as a conversation with God. What does He say to you as you read this psalm? What do you want to say to Him in response?

3. Begin a self-search in God's presence, using the follow-
    ing questions: You may think of other questions for re-
    flection as you enter this time with God:

    How do I respond to being ignored?

    How do I handle a mistake?

    How do I feel in a conversation where others dominate
    and I can't get a word in?

    What "rises up within" when someone criticizes me?
    Misunderstands me?

4. Questions such as these are well-known to Christians
    familiar with spiritual disciplines as a means of spiritual
    formation. In a very real sense, the practice of paying
    attention is a discipline of the spiritual life as much as
    the more well-known disciplines of Bible study, prayer,
    fasting, keeping the Sabbath and the practice of tithing.

    An excellent source of questions for "self-search in God's
    Presence" is the *Spiritual Disciplines Handbook: Practices
    That Transform Us* by Adele Ahlberg Calhoun.[13] The au-
    thor reminds us of the reason we do spiritual disciplines;
    not to gain respect from God or from anyone else for
    that matter, but to open ourselves more fully to God,so
    He can transform us: "Spiritual practices don't give us
    'spiritual brownie points' or help us 'work the system'
    for a passing grade from God. They simply put us in a
    place where we can begin to notice God and respond to
    his word to us."[14]

12

Home Where We Belong

Already he was a very different hobbit from the one that had run out without a pocket handkerchief from Bag End long ago. He had not had a pocket handkerchief for ages. He loosened his dagger in its sheath, tightened his belt, and went on.
–J.R.R. Tolkien[1]

My people will abide in a peaceful habitation, in secure dwellings, and in quiet resting places. (Isaiah 32:18)

When I was a little girl, I was left behind at church. I have no recollection of it, but my father assures me it happened. Apparently after everyone else had reached home that Sunday, someone realized that I was missing. Being left behind was always possible with five children in the family and it was especially possible on the Sundays when our parents drove both cars to church. On the two-car Sundays, my father would return later than my mother who would drive home as soon as the service ended to put lunch on the table. On the Sunday I was left behind, each parent could easily have assumed that I was with the other.

My father returned to church to look for me. As he related the story to me many years later, he said, "I will never forget your face peeping around the corner of the building after I called your name." I was telling this story to a friend sometime later and in the telling mentioned that I had no memory of it. My friend is a counselor, so I was not surprised when she asked with a hint of alertness in her voice, "How does it make you feel when you think about this?" I laughed at her sudden change to counselor-mode but thought about the question seriously and answered honestly, "It makes me feel wonderful. My father came for me."

Five similar words capture the essence of the gospel message: Our Father came for us. Just as my earthly father came back for me and brought me home, God the Father came for all humankind in the form of the Son to bring us home where we belong.

We are designed from the very beginning to live a certain way. A way that gives significance and security so we can live well in the world. A way that brings satisfaction to the soul and purpose to our lives. We are made to be with God, to believe Him and to bear His image. This is Life with a capital L and it is the way we are meant to live. But sin entered the world and another reality came into existence at this point. Not a God-designed reality but a sin-damaged one. We could no longer be our true selves. The real you and real me, before the Great Handover, were God-connected, God-trusting and image-bearing. After the Handover we were, and are still if we live apart from Christ, disconnected, self-serving and sin-marred. Rather than living a way that leads to life, we live a way that leads to death, without hope and without God. We are far from home and unable to return on our own.

Because God came for us and made it possible to return home, we can once again live as we are designed to live. We can be our true selves, living from the soul's deepest place of significance and responding to whatever comes our way in life from the soul's deepest place of security. We can be soul-satisfied and soul-fulfilled, because image-bearing is once again possible. In the words of Fénelon, "Those who are wholly God's are always satisfied, for they desire only that which he wills, and are ready to do whatever he requires."[2] All of this is possible when the soul returns home.

As I write this chapter, Louis and I have recently returned from another foray into the wide world. We travel extensively as international directors of a mission, and this last trip was our eleventh one this year. Each trip has been unique, adding new experiences to our "never to be forgotten" shelf of memories—walking through the night market in Taiwan and catching our first sniff of stinky tofu which is, by the way, real food and, true to its name, has a foul smell. We have had the privilege of worshiping with indigenous peoples in the Amazon, waking up to the hush of a snow-blanketed world in Switzerland, finding "Middle-earth" in New Zealand and dancing in a parade of seven thousand Africans celebrating God's faithfulness. As interesting and special as each trip is to us, however, we love coming home. Home, currently, is a small apartment on the forty-first floor of a building in Singapore called the Pinnacle. We call it our space on the top of the world.

Each time Louis and I open the door of our apartment after a long journey, there's a feeling of "rightness." As fascinating as the latest trip has been, this is where we belong, after all, not there. There's also a feeling of rest. There is rest because we've made it back once again, safe and sound, but also because we can finally lay down the weights we have carried for so long. There's the physical weight of our suitcases but also the emotional weight of immersion in places that are not only different from us in culture, language and lifestyle, but also carry their own emotions, which can be draining on the mind and heart.

When we walk into the apartment after a long trip, I usually plant my suitcase somewhere near the door and immediately walk to the large picture window of our living room and take a long, slow look. I love this view. On this last trip, we arrived home just as dawn was breaking. I looked through the window to a sky shimmering in pale hues of pink and gray. Lights were twinkling everywhere—lights of buildings and even of the boats sitting silently on a small patch of harbor that we can just barely see through a gap in the high-rise buildings which surround us. Everything was still and calm, as if dawn was saying to the world and to me, "Don't forget that there is a way to live in stillness and rest."

The dawn is right. There is stillness and rest when I am finally home and the same happens when my soul returns to its spiritual place of rest.

"The beloved of the LORD dwells in safety. The High God surrounds him all day long, and dwells between his shoulders" (Deut. 33:12).

"And he said, 'My presence will go with you, and I will give you rest'" (Exod. 33:14).

"For God alone my soul waits in silence; from him comes my salvation. He alone is my rock and my salvation, my fortress; I shall not be greatly shaken" (Ps. 62:1–2).

"My people will abide in a peaceful habitation, in secure dwellings, and in quiet resting places" (Is. 32:18).

This, too, is designer living. So we ask the question, what does a watching world see in a person who is living by God's design? It sees a soul at rest. Rest from seeking approval and worth from sources other than God. Rest from feeling unworthy from not fitting the images of beauty or success or significance that are valued in the world. Rest from anxiety and fear. Rest from a life controlled by self and all its clinging cousins. A watching world sees someone who, in the words of Kenneth Boa, is "secure enough to become others-centered rather than self-centered."[3]

The place where we are most relaxed, most comfortable, most un-needing to explain, prove, promote or defend ourselves . . . the place where we are most secure and most at rest is with God. He has designed us this way. Do you remember the list of differences between image-projectors and image-bearers from chapter five? If we live in our God-designed place of significance and security, the world will see someone who is increasingly more concerned for what God knows and thinks about him than what others know and think. It will see someone who focuses on maintaining a relationship with God rather than maintaining an image, someone who shows a secure trust in God rather than an insecure need to control and manipulate. It will see someone who is active in the world but restful in the soul.

There is rest when we come home, but there is also restoration. When Louis and I arrive at the apartment after a journey, we are well aware that our clothes have been worn too long. They looked fresh when the trip began, but after five planes and just as many airports, there is a weary and disheveled look to our travel clothes, not to mention a soured scent. The old and stained clothes need to come off and something new and fresh needs to take their place.

In the same way, the soul that has returned home needs a change of clothing. The old attire, stained with sin, has to go and we are to wear designer clothing in its place. In the world of fashion, clothing reflects a designer's signature look, whether that "look" is loose and flowing or crisp and tailored. Paul writes to the Colossians that as God's chosen people, holy and dearly loved, we are to wear compassion, kindness, humility, meekness and patience. We are to bear with each other and forgive our complaints against each other. We are to forgive as the Lord forgave us. Over all of these new coverings, Paul adds, we are to put on love to bind them all together like a belt and hold them in place (see 3:12-14). Our signature look, in other words, is the character of Christ.

To a watching world, designer living looks like rest but it also looks like Jesus. As more of Christ fills the well of our soul and more of self leaves, Christlikeness becomes the natural response to whatever situations we face and whatever people we meet. Self-life no longer rises up, because Christ-life has taken its place. In any relationship, situation, circumstance in daily life, when at that moment we live our true self in Christ, our life can be a place where others experience God's pursuing love, grace and truth touching their lives.[4]

The watching world is as large as a circle of family and friends, a neighborhood, a classroom or an office. It is as small as the clerk we encounter at a grocery store or the patient we care for in a hospital room. It is anywhere we can be image-bearers as we relate to people and respond to circumstances. An article in *Christianity Today* from June

21, 1974, quotes an excriminal named Kozlov who later became a Christian and leader of the persecuted church. As a criminal, Kozlov spent time in a Soviet prison and while there observed the Christians who shared the challenging world of prison life:

> "Among the general despair, while prisoners like myself were cursing ourselves, the camp, the authorities; while we opened up our veins, or our stomachs, or hanged ourselves; the Christians (often with sentences of twenty to twenty-five years) did not despair. One could see Christ reflected in their faces. Their pure, upright life, deep faith and devotion to God, their gentleness and their wonderful manliness, became a shining example of real life for thousands."[5]

Image-bearing brought the presence and reality of Christ into the harsh world of a Soviet prison.

David Augsberger in *The New Freedom of Forgiveness* tells another story of image-bearing. It happened during a period of history, now known as the Armenian Genocide, when Armenian peoples were being massacred by neighboring Turks of what was then called the Ottoman Empire. During this period a military unit attacked a village of Armenian Christians, killing all of the adults and small children. An officer in the raid entered a home and immediately shot the parents. He took their daughters and gave them to his soldiers, keeping the eldest daughter for himself. She remained with him for months after the raid, suffering sexual abuse and servitude until the officer became tired of her and found another girl to take her place. Eventually, she escaped the military camp, began to rebuild her life and trained to be a nurse.

One night while on duty at a Turkish hospital, the young woman was put in charge of a patient in the intensive care unit. Although he was bandaged and connected to tubes, she recognized the officer who had caused her so much suffering. The man who had murdered her parents and abused her body now needed her care or else he would die. This could well have been an opportunity for revenge. Instead, she cared for the officer through a long and difficult recovery. Eventually he recovered enough to be aware of the person who was caring for him and recognized who she was. It was not long before he spoke.

"We have met before, haven't we?"

"Yes," she replied, "we have met before."

"Why didn't you let me die when you had the opportunity? You would have had every chance, every right to kill me, would you not?"

"No, I would not," she said, "because I am a follower of Him who said, 'Love your enemies.'"[6]

Mercy like this is not a natural response when someone has suffered as much as this young woman had suffered at the hands of the patient in her care. Bitterness and hate could easily have given a motive for providing inadequate nursing care. Yet this young woman had no need for revenge, even against someone who had hurt her so terribly. She lived from the inside out and, on the inside, she was at rest. Christ shaped her thinking and in turn shaped the way she lived.

Reading a story like this is deeply challenging. Especially when we find it hard to forgive someone who has done far less to hurt us. But there is hope as well as challenge. On the map of spiritual formation, there are two red dots that shape our journey. Both are marked "You are here." The red dot of imperfection and weakness keeps us humble. It is obvious every day that all does not yet gleam in glory. But our brokenness is only half of the story. The red dot of "No longer I, but Christ" keeps us hopeful. Christ lives in you and in me, and the Spirit is transforming us into His likeness. We have all we need to live as we are meant to live if we will only pay attention to the Spirit's work and bring ourselves moment by moment to God for transformation.

"All does not yet gleam in glory," wrote Martin Luther. This sentence is part of a longer statement that Luther made on the spiritual life as a process. The full quote reads: "This life therefore is not righteousness, but growth in righteousness, not health, but healing, not being but becoming, not rest but exercise. We are not yet what we shall be, but we are growing toward it, the process is not yet finished, but it is going on, this is not the end, but it is the road. All does not yet gleam in glory, but all is being purified."[7]

Annie Johnson Flint wrote a poem that also encourages us in the process. The poem reminds us where we are to look while we make this journey to wholeness:

> I don't look back: God knows the fruitless efforts,
> The wasted hours the sinning, the regrets;
> I leave them all with Him Who blots the record,
> And mercifully forgives, and then forgets.
>
> I don't look forward, God sees all the future,
> The road that, short or long, will lead me home,
> And He will face with me its every trial,
> And bear for me the burdens that may come.
> I don't look round me: then would fears assail me,

So wild the tumult of earth's restless seas;
So dark the world, so filled with woe and evil,
So vain the hope of comfort or of ease.
I don't look in; for then am I most wretched;
Myself has naught on which to stay my trust;
Nothing I see save failures and short-comings,
And weak endeavors crumbling into dust.
But I look up—into the face of Jesus
For there my heart can rest, my fears are stilled;
And there is joy, and love, and light for darkness,
And perfect peace, and every hope fulfilled.[8]

Looking into the face of Jesus, we see the real God. And what happens when the real you meets the real God? The answer is real change. The answer is also coming home to where we belong and finding rest for the soul. We belong *to* God and belong *with* Him, each day of life on earth and for eternity. When we grasp the truths of our createdness, we no longer have spiritual amnesia. We remember who we are and how we are meant to live. When we grasp the truth that an indwelling Christ makes it possible to *be* who we are meant to be and to live as we are meant to live, we find hope for the process. We also discover a profound rest of the soul, like the rest that one feels when finally home after a long journey. The soul gratefully kicks off the ill-fitting shoes that were endured for the sake of appearance and becomes molded once again to the slippers that were made for its feet. It sinks onto the couch with a satisfied smile, because it is finally home.

Real Life with a Real God

"Make two homes for yourself, my daughter. One actual home and a spiritual home which you carry with yourself always."–Catherine of Siena[9]

1. Home is where we belong and our soul's home is with God. The following verses tell us something about the soul. What is the soul designed for according to each verse?

    Deut. 10:12–13

    Ps. 62:1,5

    Ps. 63:1–8

    Ezek. 18:4

2. How do we find rest and restoration for the soul according to each of the following verses?

Ps. 23:1–3	Jer. 6:16
Ps. 98:19	Matt. 11:28–29
Isa. 55:2	Matt. 16:24–26

3. Read Psalm 84 which reflects the idea of home and of being on journey at the same time. Use this Psalm for conversation with God and as a prayer. What does God say to you as you read? What do you want to say to Him in response?

Notes

Acknowledgements

1. Chaim Potok, *The Promise* (New York, Fawcett Crest, 1969), 171.

Introduction

1. F. B. Meyer, *Christ in Isaiah* (Fort Washington, PA: CLC Publications, 1995), 29.

2. François Fénelon, *The Best of Fénelon: Spiritual Letters, Christian Counsel, Maxims of the Saints* (Gainesville, GA: Bridge-Logos Publishers, 2002), 14.

3. Anonymous, 17th Century, Found in an English Church, "Old Nun's Prayer," *Thomas More Center*, accessed 12 July 2014, http://www.thomasmorecenter. org/Resources/Prayers/OldNunsPrayer/tabid/1529/ Default.aspx.

4. Amy Carmichael, *Mountain Breezes: The Collected Poems of Amy Carmichael* (Fort Washington, CLC Publications, 1999), 11.

Chapter 1

1. Oswald Chambers, *My Utmost for His Highest*, "The Vision and the Verity," RBC Ministries, accessed 12 July 2014, http://utmost.org/classic/the-vision-and-the-verity-classic/.

2. Augustine, *Confessions*, Book One, Chapter 1,
    Christian Classics Ethereal Library, accessed 12 July
    2014, http://www.ccel.org/ccel/augustine/confessions.
    iv.html.

3. Sadhu Sundar Singh, *With and Without Christ* (New
    York: Harper Brothers, 1929), 146.

4. Robert S. McGee, *The Search for Significance: Seeing
    Your True Worth Through God's Eyes* (Nashville: Thomas
    Nelson, 1998), 7.

5. Amy Carmichael, from *Gold by Moonlight* quoted in *I
    Come Quietly to Meet You: An Intimate Journey in God's
    Presence*, devotional readings arranged by David Hazard
    (Minneapolis, Minnesota: Bethany House, 2005), 424.

6. Bill and Gloria Gaither, "Something Beautiful,"
    Gaither Music, 1971.

7. James Strong, *The New Strong's Expanded Dictionary of
    Bible Words* (Nashville: Thomas Nelson, 2001), 305.

8. Ibid., 477.

9. A. W. Tozer, *The Knowledge of the Holy* (New York:
    Harper and Row, 1961), 97.

10. Strong, *Expanded Dictionary*, 509.

11. McGee, *The Search for Significance*, 19.

12. Amy Carmichael, *Rose From Brier* (CLC Publications,
    Fort Washington, PA, 1933), 24.

13. Hannah Whitall Smith, "July 23: Belonging and
    Becoming," in *God is Enough*, ed. Melvin E. Dieter and
    Hallie A. Dieter (Xulon Press, 2003), 149.

Chapter 2

1. George MacDonald, *The Marquis of Lossie*. Project Gutenberg, (1877) 2004, 15. E-Pub. http://www.gutenberg.org/ebooks/7174.

2. François Fénelon, *The Royal Way of the Cross*, ed. Hal M. Helms (Brewster, Mass.: Paraclete Press, 1982), 56.

3. Amy Carmichael, *Though the Mountains Shake* (New York: Loizeaux Brothers, 1946), 11–12.

4. This inspirational story is recorded in *Christian Reader*, September 1, 2001.

5. Strong, *Expanded Dictionary,* 334.

6. Dietrich Bonhoeffer, *Life Together*, quoted in Marjorie J. Thompson, *Soul Feast: An Invitation to the Christian Spiritual Life* (Louisville, KY: Westminster John Knox Press, 2005), 26.

7. Augustine, *Confessions*, Book 10, Chapter 26, *Christian Classics Ethereal Library*, accessed 12 July 2014, http://www.ccel.org/ccel/augustine/confess.xi.xxvi.html#xi.xxvi-p0.2.

Chapter 3

1. Hannah Whitall Smith, *God is Enough*, 149.

2. Strong, *Expanded Dictionary*, 418.

3. Kenneth Boa, *Conformed to His Image: Biblical and Practical Approaches to Spiritual Formation*, (Zondervan: Grand Rapids, Michigan, 2001).

4. Ibid., 715.

5. J. I. Packer, *Rediscovering Holiness: Know the Fullness of Life With God* (Ventura, CA: Regal, 2009), 11-12.

6. Jerry Bridges, *The Pursuit of Holiness* (Colorado Springs, CO: NavPress, 2003), 30.

7. Quoted in Packer, *Rediscovering Holiness*, 18.

8. Ibid., 25.

9. Strong, *Expanded Dictionary*, 544.

10. Ibid., 807.

11. Ibid., 692.

12. Ibid., 862.

13. George MacDonald, *David Elginbrod*, Project Gutenberg (1863) 2000, 2013. 216, E-pub. http://www.gutenberg.org/ebooks/2291.

Chapter 4

1. C. S. Lewis, *Mere Christianity* (NY: HarperCollins Publishers, 1952/2001), 47–48.

2. Carolyn Arends, *Theology in Aisle Seven: The Uncommon Grace of Everyday Spirituality* (Carol Stream, Illinois: Christianity Today, 2012), 233. Kindle e-book.

3. Dietrich Bonhoeffer, *Temptation* (Norwich, United Kingdom: SCM Press, 1955), 25.

4. David Benner, *The Gift of Being Yourself: The Sacred Call to Self-Discovery* (Downers Grove, IL: IVP Books, 2004), 79.

5. Carolyn Arends, "The Grace of Wrath," *Christianity Today* 52, no. 5 (2008): 64. http://

www.christianitytoday.com/ct/2008/may/23.64.
html?paging=off.

6. Lewis, *Mere Christianity*, 56.

Chapter 5

1. George MacDonald, *Diary of an Old Soul*
   (Minneapolis, MN: Augsburg Fortress, 1994) 10.

2. Strong, *Expanded Dictionary*, 668.

3. Ibid., 857.

4. Ibid., 821

5. Ibid., 509, 798.

6. Ibid., 822.

7. Ibid., 852.

8. Adele Ahlberg Calhoun, *Spiritual Disciplines Handbook:
   Practices That Transform Us* (Downers Grove, IL: IVP
   Books, 2005). Kindle e-book.

9. Benner, *The Gift of Being Yourself: The Sacred Call to
   Self-Discovery*, 80.

10. G. K. Chesterton, *Orthodoxy*, (Public Domain). 46–47.
    Kindle e-book.

11. William Temple, *Christianity and Social Order*
    (Norwich, United Kingdom: SCM Press, 1950).

12. M. Robert Mulholland Jr., *The Deeper Journey: The
    Spirituality of Discovering Your True Self* (Downers
    Grove, IL: IVP Books, 2006), 45.

13. McGee, *The Search for Significance*, 46.

Chapter 6

1. Andrew Murray, *Daily in His Presence: A Classic Devotional from One of the Most Powerful Voices of the Nineteenth Century* (New York: Random House, 2009), 213.

2. St. Teresa of Avila, *The Interior Castle or The Mansions.* Christian Classics Ethereal Library, accessed July 12, 2014, http://nanjingcatholicchurch.weebly.com/uploads/1/8/6/3/18632072/teresa_avila_interior_castle_or_mansions.pdf.

3. J. I. Packer, *Knowing God* (Downers Grove, IL.: InterVarsity Press, 1973), 70.

4. Strong, *Expanded Dictionary*, 907.

5. Packer, Knowing God, 112.

6. Paul E. Miller, *Love Walked Among Us: Learning to Love Like Jesus* (Colorado Springs, Colorado: NavPress, 2001), 37.

7. Packer, *Knowing God*, 70.

Chapter 7

1. George MacDonald, *Unspoken Sermons* Project Gutenberg (1867) 2003. 117, E-pub. http://www.gutenberg.org/ebooks/9057.

2. Alexander Pope, "The Universal Prayer." *The World's Best Poetry*, ed. Bliss Carman, et al. (Philadelphia: John D. Morris & Co., 1904); Bartleby.com, 2012. Accessed on June 11, 2014. www.bartleby.com/360/ 4/7.html.

3. Strong, *Expanded Dictionary*, 935.

4. John of the Cross, *The Dark Night of the Soul* quoted in *The Complete Guide to Christian Quotations* (Uhrichsville, Ohio: Barbour Publishing, 2011). Google e-book.

5. Lewis, *Mere Christianity*.

6. François Fénelon, *The Royal Way of the Cross*, 53.

7. Ibid., 86.

8. George Herbert, "Love." *The Oxford Book of English Verse*, ed. Sir Arthur Thomas Quiller-Couch. (Oxford: Clarendon, 1919, [c1901]); Bartleby.com, 1999. Accessed on June 7, 2014. www.bartleby.com/101/286.html.

Chapter 8

1. Bernard of Clairvaux, *On Loving God, Christian Classics Ethereal Library*, accessed July 12, 2014, http://www.ccel.org/ccel/bernard/loving_god.txt.

2. Rosemary Ellis, "On My Mind," *Good Housekeeping*, December 2008.

3. Keith Getty and Stuart Townend, "In Christ Alone," Kingsway Thankyou Music, 2001.

4. Sylvia Gunter, *Revealing the Treasures* (Birmingham, AL: The Father's Business, 2005).

5. Boa, *Conformed to His Image*.

6. Beatrice Cleland, "Indwelt" in *The Leadership of Jesus: The Ultimate Example of Excellent Leadership*, by Campbell MacApline (Sovereign World Publishers, 2000).

7. Lilias Trotter, *Parables of the Cross* (London: Marshal Brothers, Ltd.,1890), 306. Kindle e-book.

Chapter 9

1. Martin Luther, "Sermon for the Sunday after the Feast of the Circumcision, January 4, 1540," Weimar Edition (WA), vol. 49, 9.

2. Dietrich Bonhoeffer, *Cost of Discipleship* (New York: Simon and Schuster, 2012), 59.

3. Richard Rolle, *The Fire of Love* (New York: Viking Penguin, 1972).

4. M. Robert Mulholland Jr., *Invitation to a Journey: A Road Map for Spiritual Formation* (Downers Grove, IL: IVP Books, 1993), 38.

5. Amy Carmichael, *Candles in the Dark: Letters of Hope and Encouragement* (Fort Washington, PA: CLC Publications, 1981), 208. Kindle e-book.

6. Helen Roseveare, *Living Sacrifice: Willing to Be Whittled as an Arrow* (Scotland: Christian Focus Publications, 2008), 26.

7. Ibid., 26–27.

8. Ibid., 27–28.

9. Lilias Trotter, *Parables of the Christ Life* (London: Marshall Brothers, Ltd.,1899), 20.

10. Mulholland, *Invitation to a Journey*, 22–23.

Chapter 10

1. This line is attributed to Chesterton. The American

Chesterton Society addresses questions about its origin on their website: http://www.chesterton.org/wrong-with-world/.

2. Martin Luther. "Defense and Explanation of all the Articles," Second Article (1521) quoted in *Receptive Prayer* by Grace Brame (Atlanta: Chalice Press, 1985), 119.

3. Boa, *Conformed to His Image*.

4. Fénelon, *The Royal Way of the Cross*, 21.

5. Fénelon, *Spiritual Letters to Women* (Grand Rapids, MI: Clarion Classics, Zondervan, 1984), 17.

6. Ibid.

7. Andrew Murray, *The Master's Indwelling*, (Chicago: Fleming H. Revell Company, 1896), 94.

8. Fénelon, *The Royal Way of the Cross*, 31–32.

9. Ibid., 19.

10. Ibid., 8.

11. Ibid., 37.

12. Ibid., 11.

13. Amy Carmichael, *I Come Quietly to Meet You: An Intimate Journey in God's Presence*. Devotional readings arranged by David Hazard (Minneapolis, MN: Bethany House, 1999), 463. Kindle e-book.

14. Ibid., 93.

15. Charles Spurgeon, "The Tenses," No. 2718. *The Spurgeon Archive*, accessed July 12, 2014. http://www.spurgeon.org/sermons/2718.htm.

16. Fénelon, *Spiritual Letters to Women.*

Chapter 11

1. Boa, *Conformed to His Image*, 281.

2. Mulholland, *Invitation to a Journey*, 23.

3. Ruth Haley Barton, *Strengthening the Soul of Your Leadership: Seeking God in the Crucible of Ministry* (Downer's Grove, IL: IVP Books, 2008), 16.

4. Packer, *Rediscovering Holiness*, 125.

5. Ibid., 123.

6. Ibid.

7. Thomas à Kempis, *The Imitation of Christ.* Chapter 65. *World Invisible*, accessed July 12, 2014. http://www.worldinvisible.com/library/akempis/imitation/chapter%2065.htm.

8. Mulholland, *The Deeper Journey*, 121.

9. Amy Carmichael, *Candles in the Dark*, 708. Kindle e-book.

10. Leo Tolstoy, *Pamphlets, From the Russian* (Free Age Press, 1900), 71. Google e-book.

11. Amy Carmichael, *Rose From Brier* (Fort Washington, PA: CLC Publications, 1933), 3.

12. Richard Foster, *Celebration of Discipline* (New York: HarperCollins, 2009).

13. These particular questions are a variation of questions found in the chapter on "Control of the Tongue" in *Spiritual Disciplines Handbook: Practices That Transform*

Us, by Adele Ahlberg Calhoun (Downers Grove, IL: IVPress, 2005), 186–189.

14. Ibid., 19.

Chapter 12

1. J. R. R. Tolkien, *The Hobbit* (New York: Houghton Mifflin Harcourt, 1995 ed.), 214.

2. Fénelon, *The Royal Way of the Cross,* 59.

3. Boa, *Conformed to His Image.*

4. I owe this thought to Robert Mulholland's excellent book *The Deeper Journey* and particularly his chapter on what it means to live in loving union with God.

5. From *Christianity Today,* 18. No. 19, (June 21, 1974) quoted at Preaching Today, accessed July 12, 2014. http://www.preachingtoday.com/illustrations/1998/july/3917.html.

6. David Augsberger, *The New Freedom of Forgiveness* (Chicago: Moody Publishers, 2000), 129–130.

7. Martin Luther. "Defense and Explanation of all the Articles," Second Article (1521) quoted in *Receptive Prayer* by Grace Brame (Atlanta: Chalice Press, 1985), 119.

8. Annie Johnson Flint, "Perfect Piece," in *Apples of Gold* (Sword of the Lord Publishers, 1960), 209.

9. Quoted in *Catherine of Siena,* edited, annotated and introduced by Mary O'Driscoll, (New City Press, 2005), 28. Google e-book.

PUBLICATIONS

Fort Washington, PA 19034

This book is published by CLC Publications, an outreach of CLC Ministries International. The purpose of CLC is to make evangelical Christian literature available to all nations so that people may come to faith and maturity in the Lord Jesus Christ. We hope this book has been life changing and has enriched your walk with God through the work of the Holy Spirit. If you would like to know more about CLC, we invite you to visit our website:

www.clcusa.org

To know more about the remarkable story of the founding of CLC International we encourage you to read

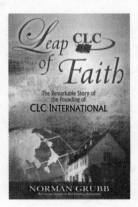

LEAP OF FAITH

Norman Grubb

Paperback
Size 5¹/₄ x 8, Pages 249
ISBN: 978-1-087508-650-7 - $11.99
ISBN (*e-book*): 978-1-61958-055-8 - $9.99